A Kentish Tale
of
Men and Manors

Eggarton Manor and Lodge.

A KENTISH TALE

of

MEN AND MANORS

James Ballingall

Illustrated by Anne Lever

PHILLIMORE

2011
Published by
PHILLIMORE & CO. LTD
Andover, Hampshire, England
www.phillimore.co.uk

ISBN 978-1-86077-701-1

Contents

LIST OF ILLUSTRATIONS

Frontispiece: Eggarton Manor and Lodge.

ACKNOWLEDGEMENTS

It is right, in a book of history, to pay tribute not only to the men and women whose bravery and roguery enliven its pages, but also to the men and women who have recorded them, and to the collectors and record-holders who preserve them. Here's then to the sword and the pen, without which this book would not have been written.

Anyone interested in the history of Kent will sooner or later (and the sooner the better) find their way to Edward Hasted. He died, in penury, in 1812, after a lifetime of research into the parishes, towns and hundreds of the County. The riches he left behind lie in his 12 volume *The History and Topographical Survey of Kent*. Our own efforts today, sitting hunched over laptops plugged into the world-wide web, seem puny and undeserving by comparison.

In the last century Hilaire Belloc, with his keen sense of history, did more than any other to rediscover and awake interest in the ancient ridgeways and pilgrim trails of the North Downs. His book *The Old Road* (published 1904) is essential reading and is quoted in the chapters that follow. I am grateful to Peters, Fraser & Dunlop on behalf of the estate of Hilaire Belloc for their permission to use this material. I am further indebted to the scholarship of I.D. Margary and his *Roman Ways in the Weald* (1948), to Collingwood and Myres and their *Roman Britain and the English Settlements*, to Philipott's *Villare Cantianum* to J.A. Giles' translation of *The Ruin of Britain* and to William Shepherd's *A Historical Atlas* (1929) which furnished me with valuable maps of Britain in times gone by. On the pages that follow you will also find lyrical evocations of village life in pre-industrial England, from the recollections of Charles Wills (1856-1929), son of the local joiner, found amongst the papers of the Godmersham Estate. He was, by trade, a coffin-maker, and by inclination, a poet. For this and other records I am indebted to the Sunley Foundation and, in particular, to John Sunley who sadly died this year before seeing any of his materials published in this book. Caroline Spencer, of Little Eggarton, provided valuable material and corrections to my Chapters on Godmersham, Michael Peters (with the archives of Chilham Castle) informed the Chapters on Chilham, while Geoff and Lindsay Oldham kindly provided access to title documentation on the Eggarton estate.

The Church, that holder of ancient truths (but with an eye on eternity) informed the chapters dealing with Godmersham Church (Canterbury Archives) and the Godmersham turnpike (Edward Knight's letter of 1830 seeking permission to cross church land), while, nearer to home, two past Vicars of St Lawrence Church Godmersham, The Rev. Walter Field and the Rev. Brade-Birks, left scholarly records and notes of the locality which I have drawn upon. Westminster Abbey allowed the use of photographs of the tombs of William and Aymer de Valence. I am also grateful to J.R.S. Phillips and his book *Aymer de Valence* for maps of the Valence Estates.

Other sources too numerous to mention here are acknowledged in footnotes to the text – designed to offer an amount of historic detail which those interested in can dwell on, while those in more of a hurry, like the pilgrims to Canterbury, can pass on by.

To peer into the past, we stand on the shoulders of those, like Edward Hasted, who have gone before. History is a collective effort, and this book has been a family affair. I am particularly grateful for the illustrations of my sister Anne Lever, which grace its pages, the IT expertise provided by my father Patrick, which inform its lay-out, the forbearance and support of my wife Sandra which underpin its writing, and the debunking offered by my three boys Hamish, Duncan and David. If this book does something to entertain, as well as instruct, if it adds a little substance to the surface of things we see today and offers some perspective to our own lives (and if it enables me to avoid dieing in penury like Edward Hasted) it will have served some purpose.

James Ballingall, July 2011

PREFACE

On a shoulder of a valley, amongst the Kentish Downs, lies the ancient seat of Eggarton.

It is situated in the Parish of Godmersham, seven miles south-west of Canterbury and six miles north-east of Ashford. An old history of Kent[1] describes it as lying in 'a wild and bleak country, consisting of barren lands and flints'. Yet this is harsh. The valley bottom, where the soil has collected over the ages, supports some farm land; not, it is true, comparable to the loamy valley of the Stour or the expanse of the Kent Weald, yet enough to sustain a settlement. Further up on the shoulder and around its wooded summit however, the chalk and flint uplands have proved stubbornly resistant to agriculture. They remain, untamed remnants of the old forest.

Our house, part of the ancient manorial estate, beautifully positioned on the hillside with swooping views down the valley, is a product of the Downs. Its roots are in the chalk, which makes up the central portion of its thick walls. Its builders used whatever materials lay to hand and, in addition to the clunch[2] hewn from nearby quarries, they added flints, bricks, and tiles. Oak boughs from the woods were used to vault the ceiling and sturdy trunks to span the floors and brace the walls.

Two Stone-Age ridge ways leading across the Downs, to Canterbury and London, pass by our house. We are flanked by Bronze-Age barrows and a Stone-Age barrow within which one of Julius Caesar's generals rests; he was part of an invasion force, fell in battle and was buried where he lay. Eggarton is named for one of the fierce Jutish invaders who flooded into the vacuum created by the passing of the Romans. In medieval times, Eggarton was caught up in battles fought between Church and State, King and the Barons, Cavaliers and Roundheads to determine the balance of power in the Land. Eggarton has been the home of men whose deeds have shaped the destiny of England, Scotland, and Wales, before laying themselves down to rest amongst the tombs of Kings in Westminster. Great historical events resonate in the bones of the hills. Knights, murderers, fraudsters, spies, pilgrims, lunatics, diarists, men of letters and captains of industry all passed this way and left their mark.

This is the story of the Kentish Downs, the events which shaped them and the characters which played their parts upon them – seen through the prism of an ancient manor.

---

1   *A New and Complete History of Kent* by William Henry Ireland 1828.
2   In former times certain types of hard chalk or 'clunch', carefully selected and capped, made a common building material in these parts.

I

Ancient Lines on the Landscape

The chalk-land Downs have been home to man from the earliest times. The first human[1] remains in this country date back some 500,000 years, and were found at Boxgrove in the South Downs. Traces of settlements not much later than this have been found in the North Downs, going back 400,000 years. In the days when a land-bridge connected Britain to the mainland, Kent was the corridor along which animals and man migrated from the continent. The chalk uplands offered safe passage and a means to navigate the dense dark forests which covered the land.

Something of that connection between the chalk landscape and the heart of man still calls to us today – as it did to Hilaire Belloc on his tramps over the Downs before the First World War, when he penned this hymn to chalk:

> The chalk is our landscape and our proper habitation. The chalk gave us our first refuge in war by permitting these vast encampments upon the summits. The chalk filtered our drink and built up our strong bones; it was the height from the slopes of which our villages, standing in a clean air, could watch the sea or the plain; we carved it – when it was hard enough; it holds our first ornaments; our clear streams run over it; the shapes and curves it takes and the kind of close grass it bears (an especial grass for sheep) are the cloak of our counties; its lonely breadths delight us when the white clouds and the flocks move over them together; where the wave break it into cliffs, they are the characteristic of our shores, and through its thin coat go the thirsty roots of our trees ... the chalk gives a particular savour to the air, and I have found it good to see it caked upon my boots after Autumn rains, or feel it gritty on my hands as I spread them out, coming in to winter fires.[2]

---

1   Homo Heidelbergensis – though a further 470,000 years was needed for it to evolve through Homo Habilis and Neanderthal to Homo Sapiens 30,000 years ago.
2   Hilaire Belloc's love of his land was not however spread equally over the country; he concludes his paean to the chalk as follows: '... the clay and the sand might be deserted or flooded and the South Country would still remain, but if the Chalk Hills were taken away we might as well be in the Midlands.' Taken from *The Old Road*.

1 (Left)   *The Stour.*

The Downs offered man vantage points which could be defended and
flints, formed from sulphurous deposits in the chalk laid
down aeons ago, which could be flaked and shaped
for weapons and tools. Though later generations
might curse the stony Kent uplands, these flinty
Downs gave man the tools to evolve from brute
Neanderthal to dexterous Homo Sapiens.

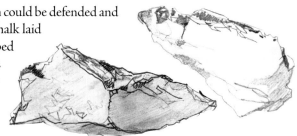

A picture of our Stone-Age ancestors can
be imagined 13,000 years ago: a small tribe of
hunter-gatherers crouched around a fire on the

2   *Flint axe heads.*

banks of the Stour, surrounded by dense pine forests, eating nuts and berries and feasting
on giant deer and aurochs, or fish and fowl from the river, sleeping in make-shift tents of
Mammoth tusks and hide. As they enjoyed their auroch steaks, however, a vast melt-water
lake, three times the size of Britain, on the other side of the world in the American heartland,
began to leak into the Atlantic sea. This cold water flow blocked off the warm Gulf Stream
which kept Britain temperate and plunged Britain into another ice age.[3] Huge glaciers crept
over the land; the hunter-gatherers retreated before them, fording an immense river (fed by the
Thames, Rhine and Seine), back over Doggerland, the land bridge joining us to the continent;
over they passed to Europe and the warmer climes of Southern France and Spain.[4] Kent was
left a frozen uninhabited wasteland. A millennium later, the climate began to warm again. The
vast glaciers retreated from the edge of the Downs, their melt-water streams carving steep sided
coombs in the escarpment as they went. Man crept back over the retreating tundra. The level
of the sea (417 feet lower than it is today) began to rise, cutting off Ireland from Britain 9,950
years ago and then in one cataclysmic moment, 8,000 years ago, breaching the land-bridge
stretching from the North Downs to the Pas de Calais.[5] The North Sea rushed in, submerging
the Dogger Bank 150 feet below the waves, and Britain became an island.[6]

In 4,000 B.C. migrants from continental Europe, brave enough to cross the channel,
came to Kent bringing with them new skills. They began to chop down the birch, alder, elm
(new species to Britain encouraged to spread by the warmer weather) and pine, making
little clearings in the forests on the flanks of the Downs. Making use of the well-drained
calcareous silty soils they began putting down roots and settling in a way unimagined by
the local hunter-gatherer population. With the cultivation of plants, such as wheat and
barley, and the domestication of animals, such as goats and sheep from the Middle East,
came the dawn of a new age: the Neolithic.

Immigration and cultural assimilation is nothing new. We need only look at ourselves
to understand this. Our DNA shows that 90 per cent of us are descended from European
hunter-gatherer stock and 10 per cent from the Middle-Eastern migrants who brought
the Neolithic farming revolution to this country – and before anyone gets too concerned
about racial purity, it is worth remembering that we are all, the world over, between
one and four per cent Neanderthal![7] Further evidence, if any such were needed, of the

---

3   The Younger Dryas.

4   This is a tradition continued today – though the preferred mode of transport is now air.

5   More precisely, the Bas de Boulonnais.

6   Not, however, for the first time. Britain had been cut off from the continent a number of times previously as
part of the cycle of ice ages and warmer ages. Some attribute the final break to have been caused by a tsunami.

7   … the rest, unless something went seriously wrong for one of our ancestors, being Homo Sapiens. *See* Ian
Morris: *Why the West Rules for Now*, March 2010.

3   *Jullieberrie Barrow.*

importance of the Downlands area to Stone-Age man can be seen in the two flint axe heads (Fig. 2), on the shelf behind my desk as I write, picked up by me from the hill above our house – and used perhaps by my Stone-Age predecessors here to clear a little space in the wood in which to make their home.

Our ancestors now began to leave other marks on the land, burying their dead in places of significance, in Long Barrows, often high above the valley floor. One such, known as Jullieberrie's barrow, lies a short walk up the valley from our house, sitting on a bluff overlooking the River Stour.

4   *The venerable beech.*

5   *Neolithic round barrow.*

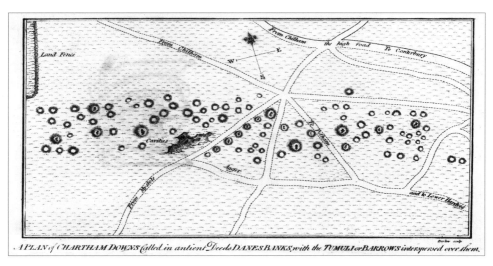

A PLAN of CHARTHAM DOWNS (called in antient Deeds DANES BANKS, with the TUMULI or BARROWS interspersed over them.

6   *Barrows on the Chartham Downs.*

The next wave of immigrants to land in Kent, in 2,200 B.C., introduced pottery and metalwork to this country and ushered in the Bronze Age. Bronze tools began to replace stone axes, and round houses and barrows replaced the hill forts and long barrows.

Two such round barrows lie on the ridge above our house hidden amongst the trees in Eggringe Wood on the eastern side of the valley. One day, whilst on a family ramble through the forest, we chanced on a clearing in which stood a venerable beech tree (*see* Fig. 4).

The glade it stood in had the feeling of a cathedral, with the trunks of adjoining trees vaulting the sky. Beyond it, in a line, were further giant beeches. It became clear that we were standing in a sacred space, laid out long ago. Following the line of trees, we came upon two Neolithic round barrows 60 feet in circumference – the resting place of some great chiefs of yesteryear. The barrows themselves were 3,500-4,500 years old, but, as remarkable, was the avenue of trees leading down, like some vast processional, to the graves. Laid down no more than 500 years ago, they are evidence that the site has been commemorated by local people in an unbroken chain over millennia.

In King's Wood, high on the western slopes of the Stour valley, there is another round barrow. If you were to stand on that, look due east, and could see through the trees which have grown up around it, your eyes would come to rest on the spire of Godmersham Church (*see* Fig. 7). If you were to ascend the spire of Godmersham Church and look due east, your eyes would come to rest on Eggarton Lodge and Manor. If you were to stand at Eggarton and look due east (and could see through trees) your eyes would come to rest on the two round barrows described above. If you were to stand on one of these barrows and look due East (and could see through trees) your eyes would come to rest on another tumulus and from there, your eyes would come to rest on the spire of Barham church.

Though we cannot look into the minds of our early forebears, we can still, at times, read their messages to us across the millennia, left on the face of the landscape. Their sacred sites and burial mounds (later, often, used by Romans, then Saxons and Normans for their own churches and graveyards), were chosen with care and precision – carefully aligned, across the landscape, with movements of sun, season or stars.

This was a thriving valley in Bronze-Age times. Just beyond Jullieberrie, north of us on the Chartham Downs lie perhaps 100 more circular Bronze-Age barrows (*see* Fig. 6).[8][9]

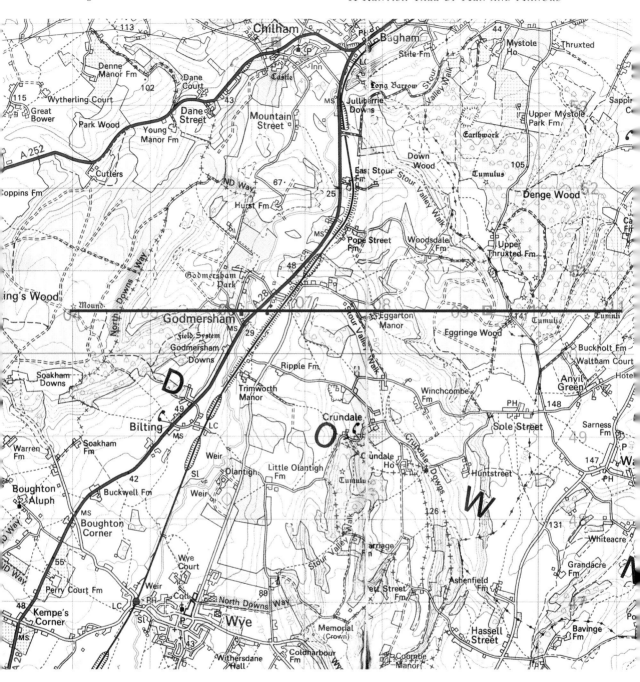

7   *Ancient lines on the map.*

8   Plan (Fig. 6) and following quote taken from Edward Hasted's *The History and Topographical Survey of Kent*, Volume 7, 1798, under Chartham: 'On the chalky downs, called Chartham Downs, adjoining the south side of the Ashford road, about four miles from Canterbury, being high and dry ground, with a declivity towards the river Stour, there are a great number of tumuli, or barrows near … Several of them have at times been opened, and the remains of bodies, both male and female, with various articles of trinkets, &c. have been found in them.'
9   Follow the purple line – from King's Wood, through Godmersham, Eggarton, Eggringe Wood – to Barham church (off the map to the east).

8   *Looking down the valley.*

Later, from 600 B.C., the Downs offered drift deposits rich in iron, near the surface, which could be quarried, to fuel man's progress from the Bronze to the Iron Age. Once again, the Stour valley was in the van, and a route developed down the valley to the Weald where wood from the forest fuelled the iron smelts. Godmersham supported a thriving Iron-Age community at this time, evidenced by the extensive field systems in Godmersham Park and lynchets on the Godmersham Downs above the church. The remains of flint, chalk and iron ore quarries can all be seen today,[10] alongside those of numerous barrows, tumuli, and hill forts. These stand testament to the history of the Downs as home to man through the Stone Age, Bronze Age and Iron Age to modern times.[11]

---

10   See, for example, quarries near the Chalk Crown on the Wye Downs.
11   For an explanation of these different eras and different types of burial site *see* Appendix 3 Part 1.

II

The Old Road

The ancient tracks, snaking along below the crest of the ridges,[1] were man's earliest thoroughfares and have served as paths to Stone-Age man, invaders, pilgrims and traders alike. These paths converge on the Wye Gap and it is no coincidence that a settlement arose near the ford in the river where these arteries come together. Along the northern slope of the Stour valley runs the ridgeway, now known as the Pilgrim's Way,[2] giving access to Canterbury for those coming from the north. On the Southern side of the valley a similar ridgeway sweeps down from the crest, through our paddock, and then on to Canterbury, providing access for those coming from the south. Running along the bottom of our valley is the Stour Valley Way providing the valley route from Canterbury, west to Wye and the Weald. The valley lies at the crossroads of a great north-south (Dover-London) east-west (Canterbury-Salisbury) axis. Eggarton, far from being a lonely outpost, lay at the heart of things in ancient times.

The Wye Gap, pierced by the Stour river through the North Downs, can be seen as the key feature in the historic landscape, through which funnel river, ridgeway, Roman road, pilgrim trail, turnpike, railway and tarmacadamed road.

Hilaire Belloc, that great champion and explorer of the chalk Downs and the paths that lie upon them, wrote of his fascination for the ancient ridgeways thus:

---

1 There were in fact often twin parallel routes – a ridge way on the top of the escarpment and a lower terrace way running just below the crest.

2 The label 'Pilgrim's Trail' was first coined in the Victorian era and began to appear on ordnance survey maps in the 1860s. It thus has no historical authenticity. For instance, Chaucer's pilgrims in the Canterbury Tales, came down from London – probably following the trail of the old Watling Street. The North Downs Way National Trail is an even more recent appellation, having been officially opened in September 1978, by the Archbishop of Canterbury at a ceremony in Wye (which, perhaps the Archbishop knew, means the 'place of the idols') two miles distant from us. What is not in doubt, however, is that these routes follow the ancient ridgeways trodden for millennia, and that these are some of the most ancient routes in Europe down which our Stone-Age ancestors made their way.

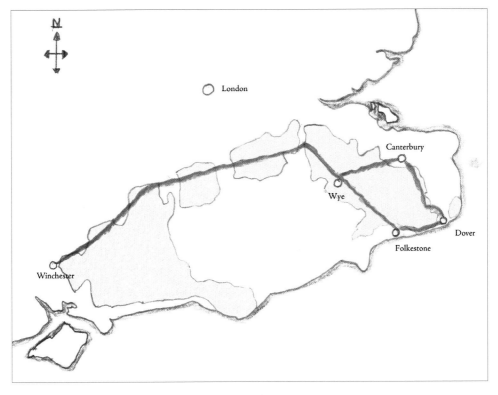

9   *The old ways.*

There are primal things that move us … of these the least obvious but the most important is The Road … it is the humblest and the most subtle … but the greatest and most original of the spells which we inherit from the earliest pioneers of our race.

He, more than any other, is responsible for retracing this most ancient of routes across the map. On a journey made at the start of the last century, before the First World War, he indulged his passion 'to plunge right into the spirit of the oldest monument of the life of man on this island'.

He called this 'the Old Road';[3] for him it had an almost mystical significance, being a kind of gift, or memory, from our forebears, imprinted on the chalk landscape. His belief in the rightness of the way was absolute. The old way never made mistakes. If you trusted to it, it would carry you across rivers, around cliffs and over marshes, finding always the safest and best route to journey's end. While false trails and cul-de-sacs withered and died, the right way would get stronger and deeper. By a process of natural selection, the right way across the landscape would evolve, born of the collective knowledge of the thousands who had gone before, leaving a genetic imprint, for those who followed, on the DNA of the landscape. In walking the Old Road you could, for a moment, engage with those travellers who had gone before and, tapping into that ancestral memory, pass in safety across the landscape, treading the same turf atop the same hills, above the same plains, beneath the same limitless sky.

---

3   He wrote about The Old Road in a book, of the same name, first published in 1904, including in it a number of fine illustrations, some of which are recorded (and adapted) in this Chapter, and for which I am indebted.

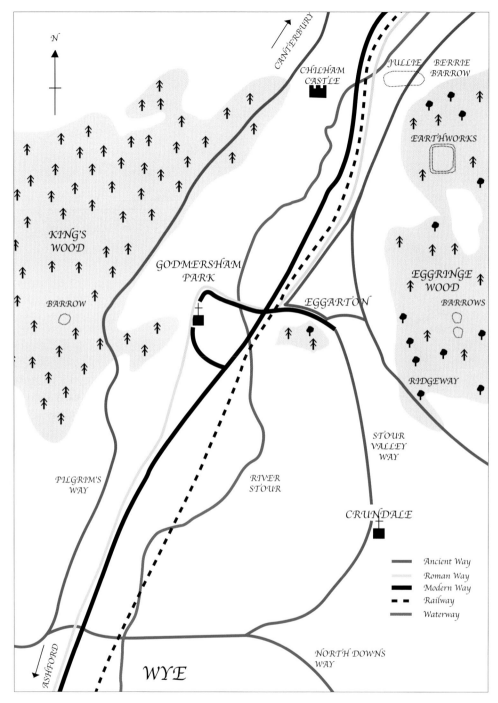

Routes ancient and modern.

A look at the map of England shows the great ridges, with their ancient ways upon them, converging on a single point – Salisbury Plain, a vast chalk plateau, with Stonehenge at its heart. Of these anti-diluvial tracks the oldest and greatest of them all is that crossing the North Downs. This was part of the ancient transcontinental route which connected

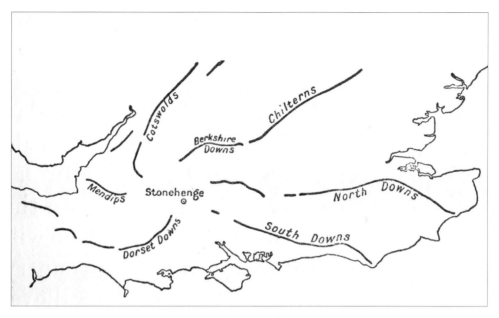

11 *The ancient ridgeways.*

us, like an umbilical cord, to the European land-mass 8,000 years ago, before the North Sea broke the land barrier and flooded into the channel. After this, the white cliffs of Dover, just visible across the swirling straits, offered the promise of landfall to early sailors, and became the gateway to the Kingdom. To those that accomplished the crossing, the ridgeway offered passage inland. From the earliest times man made his way across the Downs to the heart of England. It lays claim to be our first and oldest pathway, or indeed, as Belloc would have it, the oldest of all man-made things left to us today.

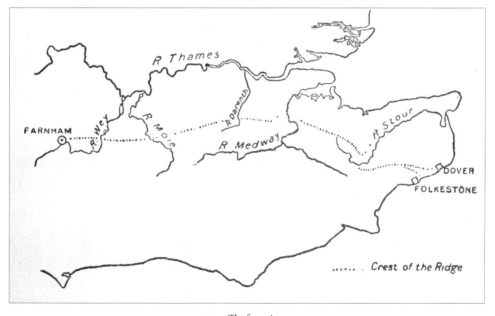

12 *The four rivers.*

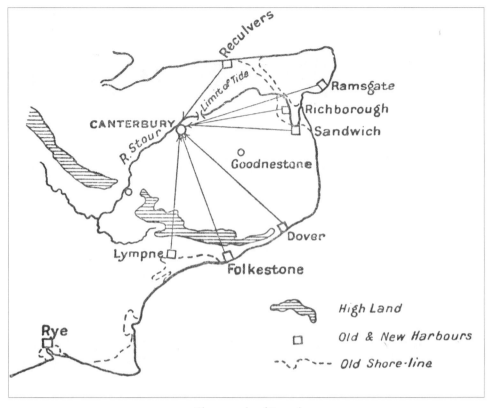

13   *The geography of Canterbury.*

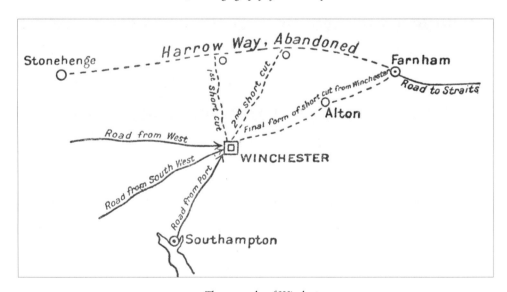

14   *The geography of Winchester.*

The Old Road existed long before the founding of Canterbury or Winchester. Indeed it was not the road which sprang from the settlements, but the settlements which sprang from the road – first of all atop the ridge itself, and later (in more secure times) in farmsteads at the base of the ridge. Later in medieval times with the twin poles of the Church (in

15   *The symmetry of the way.*

Canterbury) at one end and State (first in Winchester and later in London) at the other, settlements evolved as staging posts along the way, like a string of beads, to ease the journey of Bishop or King. If the great white Downs were the exposed bones, or spine, of the land, the Road was its nervous system, the rivers its veins and Salisbury Plain its heart.

Yet the road starts at Canterbury, a day's march from the coast, at one end, and at Winchester, a day's march from Southampton Water, at the other. The explanation for this lies in geography. In the earliest times the voyage from the Pas de Calais to the cliffs of Dover was a dangerous one; none but the most skilled of sailors dared undertake it (a fact which has protected these lands from invasion[4] many times over the ages and allowed Britain its unique history, separate from that of Europe). Those that did attempt the passage were subject to the treacherous tides and currents which funnelled down the channel. They may have aimed for the white cliffs, yet still ended up at any one of six landfalls dotted along the coast. From each of these Canterbury, on the banks of the Stour, at the limit of the tide, was the focal point. Boats could ride the salt tide up the Stour to this high-water mark, or soldiers could march a day inland, to where fresh water could be drunk. At this juncture, where all paths met, Canterbury was born.

Further down the coast, traders or visitors from Europe might make another, longer, crossing across the channel, aiming for shelter and harbour behind the Isle of Wight. Thus Winchester, like Canterbury, grew up a day's march inland from the coast, on the banks of the River Itchen at the limit of the saltwater tide. While the old way marched across the plains from Stonehenge, the gravitational pull of Winchester (the economic and political capital of Wessex) soon pulled the way south, down from its original axis.

---

4   From Romans (initially), Spanish, French and Germans.

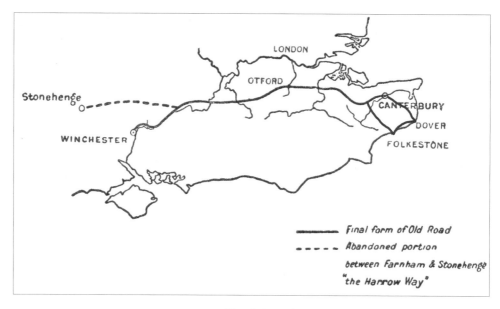

16   *The pilgrim trails.*

There is a symmetry to the geography of the Old Road. It is plain to see – with the Old Road stopping just short of the coast, on the banks of a river, at each end. There is a symmetry to its history too; it has always connected two poles of the Kingdom – the spiritual and the temporal. In ancient times Stonehenge, at its western end, was the spiritual, and Canterbury, at its eastern, the temporal.

Then the Romans came and, under the weight of their 400-year rule, the old gods were crushed and disappeared into the shadows. Stonehenge lost its authority and later, when Saint Augustine came on his great mission to convert Aethelberht, 'Britain-ruler' and King of the Saxons, to Christianity, the poles were reversed: Canterbury at one end became the spiritual centre of the country, while Winchester, at the other end, became the secular.

With the current reversed, a great tide of humanity still flowed along it, like an electric charge, but those in search of salvation now travelled east, while those in search of wealth travelled west. After some while, however, the centre of commercial and, later, royal, power moved from Winchester to London, on the River Thames. A new route then grew up, from London in the north, down the River Darrent to Otford, then along the shoulder of the Downs once more to Canterbury, in the east, or Dover, to the south; and where is the cross roads for these two great arteries of communication? Why at Wye, just over a mile from Eggarton Manor.

III

OF HOLLOWAYS AND OTHER WAYS

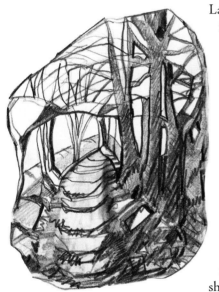

Later, when man began planting crops and farming, it was to the fertile silty lands around the rivers, where they broke through the down-land ridge, that they turned. Communities sprang up around the River Medway, and, less than a mile away from us, the Great Stour.[1] During this period the South Downs were cleared of forest and took on the smooth rolling aspect we see today, while the crests of the North Downs, with their scrubby uplands and clayey soils, proved impervious to agriculture and retained their ancient aspect.

Today 20 per cent of the Kentish Downs remains forested and, of this, 70 per cent is ancient wood, with its oak, hornbeam, ash, yew and beech.[2] These trees could be coppiced to offer poles, stakes, and lathes. Chestnut, ash, willow and maple made the long (18 foot) best-grade poles; oak, red birch, beech, cherry and hornbeam went for ordinary-grade poles; hazel, ash and oak supplied sturdy shorter stakes, hazel was preferred as lathes for the wattle and daub walls, and oak and birch went for props to the mines.

With clunch for building, chalk for slaking,[3] springs for drinking, flints for cutting, iron for farming, grass-lands for grazing, wood for burning, coppice for fencing, timber for building, barrows for burying and ridges for defending, the Downs supplied all early man's needs.[4]

---

1   Traces of a pre-historic field system, betrayed by its banks and ditches, can still be found in Godmersham Park and, on a walk up the river towards Chilham, the boundary between the Park and King's Wood.

2   This is the second highest concentration of ancient forest to be found on conservation land in England (second only to that of the Kent Weald). See especially the remnants of ancient forest at Denge Wood, above Jullieberrie, Iffen Wood just beyond at Chartham, and King's Wood on the north side of the Stour. Both Iffen Wood and King's Wood also have Bronze-Age round barrows.

3   For lime which then went for mortar, render, plaster or lime wash.

4   Later, in the 17th to 19th centuries, this coppicing tradition helped Kent supply one third of England's hop acreage. Hops needed poles to grow up. Originally the poles were grown from oak and alder, but later

17   *The gentle woods.*

Kent remained the gateway to England from the continent. Each invader from the Celts, through the Romans, Angles, Saxons, Danes, and finally Normans, would land on its coast and travel north up the spine of the Downs. Only when the lowland forests were cleared and wheeled transport replaced foot and horse did the flatter routes of the plains and valleys take over, consigning the ancient routes to the backwaters of history.

The North Downs have resisted the passage of time. Progress has transformed the dense forest of the Wealden plains into farmland, and trains and trunk roads have changed the river corridors into arteries of communication, with rushing traffic moving between the great centres of London and Canterbury; few roads, however, penetrate the irregular uplands of the Kent Downs. Those that do tend to come to an end at the head of the valley in an ancient settlement: they are not 'through' roads but 'to' roads.

You have only to venture out along the track of Eggringe Wood above our house on a wild and windy evening, past the tumuli to the Long Barrow at Jullieberrie and the ancient forest at Denge Wood, to understand that these ways belong to a bygone era. It is not until you descend from the ridge to the farmlands of the Great Stour, making its gently winding way to Canterbury, and see the rush of traffic on the Canterbury road, or cross under the branch railway line from Ashford, that you return to the 21st century.

Spanish chestnut was preferred. This accounts for many of the stands of sweet chestnut seen across the North Downs today. At its peak, 60 million poles were needed for the hop gardens, and these poles needed replacing every six years. The hop industry declined in the 20th century as tastes turned from traditional English beers to cheaper lighter lagers from abroad.

Before the advent of mechanised transport, the ridgeways of the North Downs were the main arteries of communication. Every so often a track drops down from the ridgeway routes to the valley below. These are the drovers' tracks linking the uplands to the valleys. Over the centuries, as people and animals made their way along these tracks, their passage was carved deeper and deeper, until they became like tunnels through the countryside, with tree branches meeting overhead to conceal their whereabouts.

You can still stumble on these channels, or holloways, in the Downs (*see* overleaf). One, sunk some 25 feet deep beneath the surface of the landscape, worms its way up from Eggarton Lane and comes to an end at a curious flattened area above our house. An ancient ridgeway sweeps down from the hill's crest to meet it just at this point. The holloway has sunk out of view and mind. It is now deserted, but that lane and, I believe, that flattened platform tell of peoples' lives and journeys in times past.

Hilaire Belloc felt the call of this past as an almost religious compulsion:

> To study something of great age until one grows familiar with it and almost to live in its time, is not merely to satisfy a curiosity or to establish aimless truths: it is rather to fulfil a function whose appetite has always rendered History a necessity. By the recovery of the Past, stuff and being are added to us; our lives which, lived in the present only, are a film or surface, take on body – are lifted into one dimension more. The soul is fed. Reverence and knowledge and security and love of a good land – all these are increased or given by the pursuit of this kind of learning …

18   *The wild woods.*

IV

THE COMING OF THE ROMANS

Julius Caesar landed in Britain with his Seventh and Tenth legions in 55 B.C.[1] Having conquered Gaul over the previous three years (adding France and Belgium, together with large parts of Holland, Germany and Switzerland, to the Roman Empire) he felt in need of a new challenge. Annexing Britain, he calculated, should add further lustre to his reputation, setting him up to assume sole control of the Republic (instead of having to share it with Pompey and Crassus).[2] Besides, the Britons had a nasty habit of supporting the Gauls, who were revolting enough as it was, and needed to be taught a lesson. Unfortunately this, his first encounter with the Britons, could not be described as a triumph even by Caesar (who invariably put the most optimistic gloss possible on events in his reports home). Caesar, the most famous of men, almost ended his days on a lonely windswept strand off the Kentish coast.[3]

Immediately after Caesar landed a storm brewed up and smashed his boats on the beach.[4] The Britons, meanwhile, adopted the strategy of falling on the Romans whenever they saw a convenient opportunity and then, having been beaten off, pretending it had all been a mistake and suing for peace. After this had happened a couple of times Caesar became fed up with the whole business, packed up his troops in his salvaged boats, together with a few hostages for good measure, and set sail back to Gaul. The Britons, watching him leave from the cliffs, thought they had beaten him – but they did not know the man.

---

1   Probably at Walmer, the sea coast of the 'weallas' or slaves (though named by the Saxons not Romans).
2   The other two Triumvirs.
3   *De Bello Gallico* Book 4, chapters 20 to 36. To be fair, Julius Caesar probably never intended his first expedition to be more than a reconnaissance – but it still almost ended in disaster.
4   Caesar, rather lamely, blames this uncharacteristic blunder on the high tide of a full moon. More likely, however, used to the small tides of the Mediterranean, he was simply caught out by the bigger tides of the Atlantic and failed to haul his boats far enough up the shore.

19 (LEFT)   *Ancient holloway.*

Caesar was a man who felt destiny's stamp upon him; he could not brook this affront by the Britons. From the other side of the straights he immediately set his shipwrights to work on an invasion fleet – an armada of 600 ships. In true Roman style this was ready in less than a year and Caesar, once again, prepared to set sail – not with two legions this time, but with five.[5] Again mother-nature smiled on the Britons and sent a powerful easterly wind to blow his ships past the Kentish headland and off towards the North Sea. Caesar, however, had learned his lesson from before and had designed his boats with oars as well as sails this time. Thus it was that, by dint of some heavy rowing, he finally came within sight of the Kentish coast again. The Britons, temporarily united under King Cassivelaunus, in true untrustworthy fashion, had stood on the cliffs and jeered the previous day as his armada was washed out to sea. When they saw it reappearing over the horizon the next morning, however, they thought it wise to beat a retreat and hide in the woods. Later that day therefore when Caesar made landfall,[6] he was surprised to find his legions unopposed. Ever one for decisive action, he left his ships riding at anchor off the coast (not risking beaching them on the shore after the previous year's debacle) and made a forced march that night, driving in from the coast, 12 miles north. Dawn found him on the Downs,[7] on a hillside over-looking the Stour, under heavy rain.

At first light a horseman came cantering up the slope to report (as his diary relates): 'a very great storm having arisen, almost all the ships were dashed to pieces and cast upon the shore, because neither the anchors and cables could resist, nor could the sailors and pilots sustain the violence of the storm.' Caesar was a greater general than an admiral. Again he had underestimated the power of the Atlantic. As Simon Schama put it in his memorable phrase: 'History always fought on the side of the Romans. But, as it turned out, Geography did not.'[8] The loss of a fleet meant the loss of passage home. Caesar could not let this pass and, taking a troop of men, returned to the beach to survey the wreckage, leaving his main force vulnerable on the flanks of the Jullieberrie Downs.

As soon as Caesar's back was turned the Britons came charging out of the woods. Thus the legionaries found themselves cold, wet, far from home, still queasy from the crossing and ambushed by a force of savages storming down the hill, some on horse, some in chariots, wheeling around them in full battle cry.

Now, if ever, was the time for the legionaries to show their metal. These were, after all, men, never bested in battle, teak hard from three years' campaigning in Gaul. They assumed their battle formation[9] under the orders of Quintus Laberius Durus, marshal in the field. The Britons attacked: the line held. Unable to break them, the Britons eventually wheeled off back into the woods[10] and disappeared as suddenly as they had come, leaving the legionaries to bury their leader, where he fell. Reputedly he lies there still, entombed in the Jullieberrie Downs

---

5   25,000 men, plus 2,000 cavalry. The invasion, however, nearly never took place. Legionaries were better soldiers than sailors and, remembering the storms and landing of the previous crossing, at first refused to board ship.

6   Possibly at Lymen, though opinions differ.

7   Above our house.

8   Simon Schama, *A History of Britain: At the edge of the World*, p.28.

9   The 'testudo' or tortoise.

10   The guerrilla tactics of the Britons though effective against stragglers were never a match for the battle formations of the Roman army.

(named after him),[11] in an ancient grave within a still more ancient long barrow overlooking the Stour at Chilham.[12]

The alternative explanation for this barrow, favoured in medieval times, is that it is the resting place for the bones of a great giant called Jullaber. Roman burial remains, covered by flints, have been found on the south side of the Jullieberrie barrow, together with a horde of Roman coins; as yet, however, no remains of a giant have been found. The reader may choose which explanation he prefers.

Caesar, having ordered the repair and re-provision of his navy, returned and forced the crossing of the Stour. With his Seventh legion, he attacked the Britons in their hill-fort at Bigbury, overlooking the Stour Gap on the other side of the river, and then made his own camp at nearby Chilham.[13]

Caesar went on to cross the Thames and penetrate into the heart of the country, but he was never able to say of Britain (as he had of Pontus):[14] 'I came, I saw, I conquered.'[15] In the end, however, it was a Gaul, Vercingetorix, the leader of rebellious tribes in the South of Gaul, who saved Britain. Caesar, hearing news of this rebellion brewing in the Auvergne, realised he was at risk of losing one empire for the sake of gaining another – and decided to withdraw.

Thus once again the Britons were able to watch Caesar, from the safety of the cliffs of Dover, depart across the water – albeit with some hostages and promises of tribute ringing in his ears.[16] It was to be a further hundred years before the Roman Eagle again cast its shadow on the Kentish Downs.

In true untrustworthy British fashion, however, the Britons stopped paying tribute as soon as they deemed it safe to do so – shortly after he had disappeared over the horizon.[17]

---

11   Local tradition perhaps conflated or confused the names of Julius Caesar, the Commander, with Laberius Durus, his Tribune, to make Jullieberrie.

12   Philipott in his *Villare Cantianum*, 1659, at p.117 offers an explanation as follows: 'There is a place in this Parish [Chilham] on the South-side of the River stretched out on a long green Hill, which the Common People (who bear the greatest sway in the corrupting of Names) call Jelliberies Grave. The Historie itself will evidence the original of this denomination. It was about this place that Julius Caesar respited his farther remove or advance into the bowels of this Island, upon intelligence received that his Fleet riding in the road at Lymen not far distant, had been much afflicted and shattered by a Tempest; whereupon he returned, and left his Army for ten dayes, encamped upon the brow of this Hill, till he had new careen'd and rigged his Navy; but in his march from hence was so vigoriously [*sic*] encountered by the Britons that he lost with many others Leberius Durus, Tribune and Marshal of the Field, whose Obsequies being performed with solemnities answerable to the eminence of his Place, and Command, each Souldier as was then Customary, bringing a certain quantity of earth to improve his plane of Sepulture into more note than ordinarie, caused it so much to exceed the proportion of others elsewhere; and from hence it assumed the name of Julaber, whom other vulgar heads, ignorant of the truth of the story, have fancied to have been a Giant, and others of them have dreamed to have been some Enchanter or Witch.'

13   *See further* Chapter 19.

14   An area of Northern Turkey, bordering the Black Sea.

15   Or, in his own words: 'Veni, vidi, vici.' He was a man, clearly, whose good opinion was hard to earn. On the whole, however, perhaps it is better to be thought untrustworthy, than weeny, weedy and weak (*pace* Sellar and Yeatman).

16   The Ninth Century *Anglo Saxon Chronicle* (a counterpoint to Caesar's own *De Bello Gallico* and an example, for once, of history written by the losers) describes Caesar's expeditions thus: 'Sixty winters ere that Christ was born, Caius Julius, emperor of the Romans, with eighty ships sought Britain. There he was first beaten in a dreadful fight, and lost a great part of his army. Then he let his army abide with the Scots, and went south into Gaul. There he gathered six hundred ships, with which he went back into Britain. When they first rushed together, Caesar's tribune, whose name was Labienus, was slain. Then took the Welsh sharp piles, and drove them with great clubs into the water, at a certain ford of the river called Thames. When the Romans found that, they would not go over the ford. Then fled the Britons to the fastnesses of the woods; and Caesar, having after much fighting gained many of the chief towns, went back into Gaul.' It is believed that reference here to Labienus was an erroneous interpretation of an original shorthand Latin reference to Laberius.

17   A policy adopted once again more recently by Margaret Thatcher when she renegotiated our payment of dues to the EU in 1984.

V

The Second Coming of the Romans

The Britons had been able to see off the Romans and, perhaps, kid themselves that they had won the day. Rome, however, had a long memory. So far as its Emperors were concerned, the conquest of Britain remained very much 'unfinished business'.

This affront to Roman power echoed down the decades until, nearly a hundred years later, a subsequent Emperor, Claudius, answered its call and determined to add Britain to his Empire. Once again Kent was the key, though Claudius, having read his *De Bello Gallico*, realised this time the importance of finding a safe harbour. Thanet, now a part of mainland Britain, was then an island cut off by the Wantsum channel, and offered an ideal harbour for a fleet such as Claudius'. He chose a gentle beach off the Wantsum channel, which promised an easy landing and shelter from storms. So it was that in A.D. 43 four Roman legions, 40,000 men, and horse set foot once more on British soil at Richborough. This time they were unstoppable.

From Richborough (or Rutupiae as the Romans called it) they marched west-north-west up the shoulder of the Downs (as all invaders, before or since, have done). The Britons were caught unprepared. They had heard tell, from the Belgi across the straights, of the legionaries' mutiny in Bologne and concluded that the invasion would never happen.[1] They had fatally underestimated their opponents. They fell back.

News of the landing spread. Caratacus (one of the tribal Kings) assembled his men and sought some vantage point to make his own. The lines of the rivers in Kent had ever served as defence against invaders. Caratacus made his stand, perhaps on Caesar's old battle ground, the Stour, but the legionaries brushed him aside. He retreated to the line of the Medway, where he regrouped and joined forces with his brother Togodumnus. Here the Britons met the full force of the Roman war machine. The battle raged for two days, but eventually the legionaries, under their General Plautius, won the day. This was the

---

1   The legionaries were better soldiers than sailors. In those days crossing the channel was a hazardous venture, and they still remembered the trials that had beset Caesar on both his crossings. Eventually the troops were won over, however, and the armada set sail.

turning point of the campaign. The Romans gained the ridge above the river only to spy the Britons disappearing across the plain: Britain lay open before them.

Unlike Caesar, Claudius thought it wise to lead his army from the comfort of his own home in Rome, and only venture forth when all the dirty work had been done. On receiving word from Plautius, therefore, Claudius set out from Rome, suitably escorted by a contingent of his Praetorian guard and a squad of elephants. He arrived in time to cross the Thames and claim the victory. Claudius had succeeded where the mighty Caesar had failed. No doubt the rather diminutive club-footed Emperor[2] allowed himself a little smirk of satisfaction as he led the triumph into his new capital, Colchester, perched, rather incongruously, behind the ears of his imperial pachyderm.

Sixteen hundred years later, the memory of those beasts (the first such to visit these shores since the days of the woolly mammoth) lived on. In 1668, villagers in Chartham were sinking a new well into the chalk. Seventeen feet down they came upon 'monstrous bones together with four teeth … petrified and turned into stone … each as big as the fist of a man'.[3] Opinion was divided as to whether these were the remains of elephants, brought over to Britain as part of the Romans' invasion force, or of some giant marine monster.

The Romans' immediate priority was to secure their lines of communication home, and for this they needed roads. Their first and greatest road, the Watling Street, ran west-north-west from Dubrae (Dover) to Duovernum (Canterbury), their supply base; others followed from other ports, protected by great forts which they built at Lemenae (Lympne), Dubrae (Dover), Rutupiae (Richborough) and Regubrium (Reculver). The road from Lympne travels straight as an arrow from the coast to Canterbury.[4] It remains to this day, and is called Stone Street – a tribute to the surface given to it by Roman engineers. While other ways meander along the contours of the landscape, these Roman roads dissect the map like a surgeon's scalpel.

Claudius meanwhile advanced to the Thames and established his forward supply base at Londinium. From there he launched a three-pronged attack to conquer the rest of the country. Marking the progress of his legions are the three great Roman roads: Akeman Street to the west, Ermine Street to the north, and Watling Street to the north west. These they bounded by a fourth: the Fosse. This marked the initial extent of Roman ambition over the land.

Later, other roads were built and expeditions launched, and further land fell to the Romans. The native Celts were pushed to the outer edges of the island, to Cornwall, Wales and Scotland, places which, ever since, have preserved their Celtic identity and maintained a measure of independence from the rest of the land.

Perhaps the most lasting memorial the Romans left us is their road network. Set out below is a map showing the 'trunk' roads designed, presumably, for Claudius' elephants, of the early Romans in Kent, laid out boldly across the landscape and based around two parallel routes, one either side of the North Downs ridge, with two lateral connections running through the gaps made by the rivers Stour and Medway where they punctuate the ridge. (*See* Fig. 20 overleaf.)[5]

---

2   Claudius is described as follows by Suetonius: 'His knees were weak and gave way under him and his head shook. He stammered and his speech was confused. He slobbered and his nose ran when he was excited.' What he lacked in stature, however, he made up for with the size of his name: Tiberius Claudius Caesar Augustus Germanicus.

3   Edward Hasted's *The History and Topographical Survey of Kent*, Volume 7, 1798, under Chartham.

4   Capital of the Cantii and named Durovernum by the Romans.

5   *The Archeology of Kent to A.D. 800*, edited by John H. Williams 2007. The blue line is the modern county boundary.

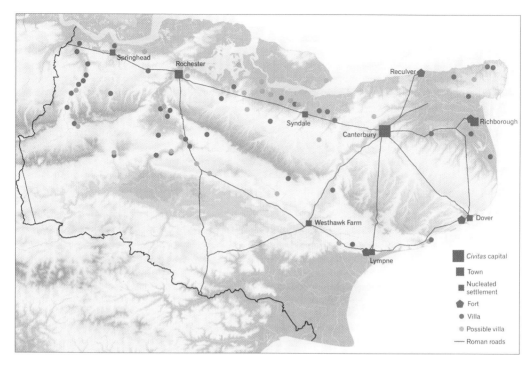

20   *Downs and roads.*

The great Roman military roads, laid out by Roman engineers as part of the invasion force, were designed for the quick movement of troops over the land. They were also a symbol of Roman power and order: the stamp of an occupying force: the mark of Rome. Hills, rivers and forests – all were subdued to the will of these engineers as they marched across the landscape. Also, for the early Roman settlers on the far flung edge of Empire, this was the umbilical cord connecting them to their heartland; for them indeed, all roads led to Rome. The nearest equivalent feat we can claim today is our network of railway lines, laid out straight across the map, connecting towns by the shortest distance, cutting through the landscape, no respecter of nature.

The Romans established their first base at Duovernum (Canterbury), broadly equidistant from the four channel ports from which their supplies would come. From Canterbury, they struck west in the steps of the army, establishing Watling Street as their main artery west to Londinium; next they built a road south-west through the Stour Gap, towards modern-day Ashford. Canterbury soon sat like a fat spider on the map of Kent, at the centre of a web of roads radiating out to the ports and other strategic footholds inland. They quickly realised the tactical importance of the River Thames and established Londinium as their forward supply base. The Watling Street swelled into a major line of communication and settlements grew up at staging points along the way at Syndale, Rochester, Spinghead and Faversham. Roman settlers and governors, following on in the legion's footsteps, built their villas on the Downs.[6]

---

6   It is clear that Romans settled on the Downs all around us. Roman remains have been found nearby on the hill east of Crundale in the parish of Godmersham. In the 18th century Rev. Brian Faussett found a number of funerary urns, skeletons, ashes, and coins there – one of which bore the name of Faustina, wife of Marcus Aurelius who died in A.D. 177. Further remains were found in the holloway, sunk down below the surface of the ground near the summit of Tremworth Downs – *see* Edward Hasted's *History and Topographical Survey*

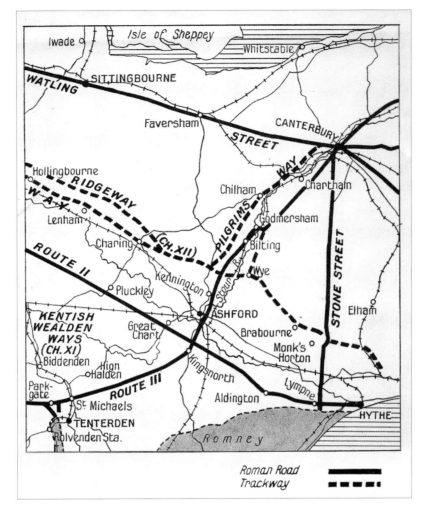

21 *Ancient Ridgeways and Roman roads.*

The later roads built by the Romans, when military demands were less pressing and commercial considerations came to the fore, were less direct and followed, to an extent, the contours of the landscape. These, rather than their more famous Streets ('via strata' or paved ways), evolving over time for the convenience of the ordinary people, were the precursors of our road system today. The road from Canterbury to Ashford is one such, connecting the iron works of Sussex to the military centre at Canterbury.[7] In Sussex the road was metalled with slag iron from the foundries, while in Kent the surface was more usually of flint and stone.

Once again Godmersham, with its strategic location at the point of a ford over the Stour river, was at the heart of things. The detailed map at Appendix V shows a section of the

of the County of Kent. Villas have been found at Ashford and at Wye (South of Harville Farm) and other Roman remains have also been found at Gottye Wood, Chilham – two miles away down the Stour valley – at Jullieberrie and Chartham (just beyond that) and in the grounds of Godmersham Court Lodge.

7   Interestingly however the Kent Archaeological Society, in its book *The Archaeology of Kent to A.D. 800,* believe that this route is arguably the most ancient of the routes and, on the evidence of recently excavated roadside settlements at Westhawk farm (where the road crosses the way from Dover and Lympne to Rochester), dates to the pre-Flavian period (before the reign of Emperor Vespasian A.D. 69-79).

22   *At the fording of the Great Stour: today.*

Roman road, connecting Canterbury to Ashford,[8] which makes its way past Godmersham and our own house at Eggarton. Once again therefore in Roman times, Eggarton, with its strategic position on the eastern side of the Wye Gap, near the fording of the Great Stour, was at the centre of things.

Here then Rome's newest province was mapped out by its engineers and soldiers and a unified England first took shape under the shadow of the Roman Eagle. For over 400 years the Britons enjoyed the 'pax Romana' – the longest period of peace ever to be enjoyed by the people of these shores; but all good things come to an end and finally the Romans left these shores in A.D. 427 – their own empire in collapse.

---

8   Originally known as Esbetisford – where many ashen trees grow about the ford.

VI

WHAT'S IN A NAME – A ROMAN POSTSCRIPT

It has been said that history is written by the winners – and so it is. Some of the biggest winners ever were the Romans. Caesar in particular felt the need to record his triumphs. His British exploits, however, earned only passing mention as part of his Gallic campaigns, and perhaps that is how he thought of them – as merely an adjunct to the main show on the mainland. His British campaigns were, after all, not his proudest moments and, were it not for the optimistic gloss he put on events, could be seen as a failure. I am sure any Briton writing at the time would have made them so.

It suited Caesar to dismiss the ancient Britons as barbarians (with the possible exception of the men of Kent, of whom he said: 'Of all the Britons the people of Kent are the most civilised.')[1] As a result, for nearly 2,000 years the ancient Britons have received a very bad press. In the Roman view of the world, there were only two types of people, Romans and barbarians, and if you were not a Roman you were a barbarian.[2]

Even today, 2,000 years later, we fall into the trap that Caesar laid for us, and, as we dig ourselves out, we realise (from the excavations we now make) that the Britons were not, after all, barbarians. From the artifacts we now find we can see that they had an advanced civilisation of their own, capable of artistry in gold, bronze and iron. They were producers, and traders, of exquisite works of art and beauty, warriors of outstanding courage and dexterity[3] and organisers of immense labour forces capable of creating extraordinary henges, earthworks and hill forts.[4] They were also followers of a religion, druidism, so powerful, that the Romans feared it and sought to extirpate it from the land and erase it from the pages of

---

1   Caesar was not a man much given to compliments, especially if you were a barbarian, so even this rather begrudging one is worth something.

2   The Emperor Claudius (who actually succeeded in conquering Britain) was as bad. He carved on his Triumphal Gate in Rome: 'Eleven British Kings surrendered. I brought British barbarians from across the ocean under the authority of Rome.'

3   Which even Caesar admitted.

4   Such as the one at Maiden Hill in Dorset – the largest in Western Europe, bigger than 50 football pitches and fortified by triple ditches and ramparts.

history. The one thing the Britons could not do, however, was write their own history (for theirs was a 'pre-historic' civilisation). But, make no mistake, the Britons, especially the men of Kent, were worth the conquest; the Romans would not have bothered were they not.

Over the years since Caesar, it has been presupposed that Britain was incapable of producing things of merit itself, without their being brought from across the waters. It has been said that our early artistry was the work of Celtic immigrants, that our civilisation was a gift from the Romans, our buildings the product of the Normans, our renaissance the work of Italy. We can trace this 2,000-year-old inferiority complex back to Caesar, but here it ends. Caesar never truly conquered Britain. We won, Caesar lost, and all the rest is sour grapes.[5]

Until the time of the Romans, Britain was a largely uncharted land, harbouring a collection of different tribes with no concept of a single national identity. This was a confusing state of affairs for all concerned, since no-one was very sure who was who.

As everyone now knows, the Celts really belong in Scotland, Wales and Cornwall, but it was only when the Romans arrived and pushed them back that they assumed their rightful position. The Romans then confused the situation again by calling them 'Picti' or 'the painted ones'. This was sheer laziness on their part since Picti was simply their all-purpose expression for any barbarian beyond the fringe of Empire. The Celts in Scotland, far from being affronted by this, rather took to this idea; thenceforth, to live up to their name, they covered themselves from head to toe in blue woad whenever they attacked the Romans – which was often. The Scots, meanwhile, had been living happily in Ireland, until, in Roman times, realising their mistake, they moved to Scotland (the land of the Picts).

Caesar, though great on history (he created lots of it), was not so strong on geography. He got things off on the wrong foot entirely by describing his wars against the Britons in a book which he called *De Bello Gallico* (thus pre-dating European union by about two millennia). He suspected there were links between the Brittani (who lived in Belgium) and the people of England. Caesar thus, mistakenly, started to call us the Brittani, when it had been decided at least four centuries earlier that we were Prittani.[6] Thus it can be seen that we are all one of Caesar's little mistakes; the Scots are really Irish, the Celts are really British, the Picts are really barbarians, and the Brits are really Belgian. Nobody, at the time, was brave enough to point this out to Caesar and so the mistake has gone on. Still, if Caesar had not fallen into this schoolboy error, we could so easily have been called the Pricks (instead of the Brits) – and, who knows, perhaps we sometimes are.

The Romans gave every country they conquered a female figure to represent it. Ours was Britannia – and she started to appear on Roman coins. Two thousand years later we can still find her on our coinage[7] and (having forgotten she was an emblem of our own oppression) we have even adopted her for our national song: Rule Britannia. As for Kent, this too was a Roman invention. They called it Cantium, which means 'the corner of land' or 'land on the edge'. The people, they called Cantii (people of Cantium) and the administrative area the 'Civitas Cantiacorum' (the state of Cantium). The precise area of the Civitas is uncertain, but it probably extended as far as the Thames in the north (perhaps even including London).[8]

---

5   For which, along with our wine, we do of course have Rome to thank.
6   A host of learned geographers four centuries earlier (Diodorus, Siculus, Strabo, and Ptolemy to name but some) had already agreed that we were Pritanni and that we lived in the Pritanic Isles. Because Caesar had launched his invasion from a place in Belgium, populated by a tribe called the Brittani, he assumed that Britain had been populated by this tribe, and that he was simply correcting an error by calling us Britons, and our land the British Isles.
7   The fifty pence piece.
8   Probably similar to the county of Kent in medieval times, almost 1,000,000 acres. The modern Kent is

23 *Roman Britain: Roman roads.*

For all their mistakes, however, it was the Romans who created the concept of Britain and for that, perhaps, we can thank them. (*See* Fig. 23.)[9]

slightly smaller following the establishment of the county of London, 1889 (which in turn was replaced by Greater London in 1965).

9   Taken from a *Historical Atlas* by William R. Shepherd, 1929 edition.

VII

GILDAS THE CROSS AND THE DARK AGES

The Romans, like the Celts and Britons before them, left their imprint on the landscape; their legacy, however, was more substantial. Instead of ridgeways on the flanks of the Downs they left roads on the face of the plains,[1] and, instead of ramparts and palisades on the high ground, they placed a wall around the neck of England, and forts along her coast[2] whose battlements, of indestructible concrete,[3] still tower over us today. In A.D. 427 however, the legionaries marched out of their forts and onto their boats, leaving the great castles empty; the Britons' defence against the seaborne raiders of the South and the Picts of the North was gone. Britain became a very frightening place.

Some historians today believe the cultural legacy of the Romans to be overstated. France and Spain owe their very language to the Romans (being, with Italian, amongst the Romance or Latin-based languages). The English language owes more to the Angles and Saxons than to the Romans, and the Celtic more to Gaelic. Evidence of Roman culture dots the French and Spanish landscapes in the form of theatres and circuses. No such cultural relics remain in Britain (only military ones). Be that as it may, the Britons in A.D. 427 felt lost without the Romans and sent emissaries to Rome for help. Their pleas fell on deaf ears. The Roman Empire, half a millennium old, could no longer defend itself against the northern hordes, let alone aid a far flung land on the edge of empire. The Britons had been abandoned. With the great Roman towns lying empty and all pretence of order or industry gone, an eerie silence fell upon the land. The people, so long dependent on the might of Rome to govern and protect them, had forgotten how to fend for themselves. The menace grew from the Picts of the north and, in the face of savage raids, the Britons slunk into the forests. The Dark Ages had begun.

---

1   Altogether 5,000 miles across the country.
2   What was once a coastal defence may now appear to be curiously placed some miles inland (for example at Pevensey). This however is attributable more to the shifting of our coastline over the millennia than to the poor surveying of the Roman engineers.
3   The Romans took the secret of their cement with them to the grave, and even today, with all our modern technology, we can scarce match it for strength and resilience.

In desperation they sought help from the brothers Hengist and Horsa of Jutland in Denmark. Around A.D. 450 the brothers sailed to their aid, but when they saw the land, they wanted it for themselves. Having defeated the Picts, they sent to their homeland for reinforcements, reporting of the worthlessness of the Britons and the excellence of their land. Three Germanic tribes answered the call and ships arrived crammed with Jutes, Saxons and Angles, bent on nothing short of total dominion. The Britons had invited wolves into the sheeps' fold, and they proved savage. Squeezed between seaborne invaders and Pictish raiders the Britons fled. Some escaped to the north, and some to the forests of North West France – which became known as Brittany (Little Britain). The darkness and despair of these times is uniquely captured in the words of a British monk called Gildas Bandonicus, or Gildas the Wise:

> The barbarians push us back into the sea; the sea pushes us back into the barbarians; between these two kinds of death we are either drowned or slaughtered.

Living a century after the departure of the legions Gildas the Wise (or Gildas the Cross as I prefer to call him, judging by the tone of his writing) lamented the condition of the country. Looking back on the Roman occupation as a golden age he set out to denounce the wickedness of his times and the impiety of his fellow countrymen. In A.D. 546, unable to contain himself any longer, he set all this down in a manuscript, which he called 'The Ruin of Britain'. This is the earliest record of these times and remains, to this day, the mother and father of all diatribes. The following will give you something of the flavour of it.[4]

He starts off with the usual sort of apologia:

> WHATEVER in this my epistle I may write in my humble but well-meaning manner, rather by way of lamentation than for display, let no one suppose that it springs from contempt of others, or that I foolishly esteem myself as better than they …

then hints of things to come:

> the subject of my complaint is the general destruction of every thing that is good, and the general growth of evil throughout the land … for it is my present purpose to relate the deeds of an indolent and slothful race.

That race, in case you are wondering, is us. According to Gildas Britain, in the good old days, was brimming with milk and honey; there was no place you would rather be:

> The island of Britain, situated on almost the utmost border of the earth, towards the South and West, and poised in the divine balance, as it is said, which supports the whole world, stretches out from the South-West towards the North pole, and is eight hundred miles long and two hundred broad … It is famous for eight and twenty cities … Its plains are spacious, its hills are pleasantly situated, adapted for superior tillage, and its mountains are admirably calculated for the alternate pasturage of cattle … It is decked, like a man's chosen bride, with divers jewels, with lucid fountains and abundant brooks wandering over the snow white sands; with transparent rivers, flowing in gentle murmurs …

---

4   For those interested in the whole unadulterated rant, these extracts are largely taken from the translation of J.A. Giles on the website at the University of Tennessee, accessed through the Internet Medieval Source Book. This is taken from the the *Saxon Parker Chronicles*, held at Parker Library, Cambridge. Although historians poor scorn on the work of the Monk Gildas – and it does compare badly to the more careful and scholarly writing of the Venerable Bede – it was never intended as a work of history and its self-confessed object was one of denunciation and exhortation. Whatever else it may be, as a picture of Britain in the Dark Ages following the retreat of the Romans, and as a record of the fall and fear of its people, it is unique.

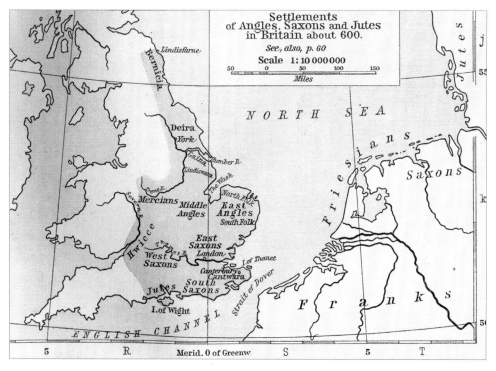

24   *Engaland: seventh century.*

You get the idea – but then, as with a still more ancient tale, a woman, Boudicca, is fingered with the cause of our downfall.[5] After Boudicca's rebellion, it was downhill all the way until the Romans, finally, decided to leave these shores and the Picts and Scots rushed in to fill the void:

> The Roman legion had no sooner returned home … than their former foes, like hungry and ravening wolves, rushing with greedy jaws upon the fold which is left without a shepherd, and wafted both by the strength of oarsmen and the blowing wind, break through the boundaries, and spread slaughter on every side.

The Britons begged for help, but to no avail:

> The Romans … left the country giving notice that they could no longer be harassed by such laborious expeditions … nor suffer the Roman Standards to be worn out by sea and land by fighting against these unwarlike, plundering vagabonds.

Rome had had enough. The Britons then made something of a tactical mistake:

> Then all the councillors, together with that proud tyrant Gurthrigern [Vortigern], the British King, were so blinded, that, as a protection to their country, they sealed its doom by inviting in among them (like wolves into the sheep-fold), the fierce and impious Saxons, a race hateful both to God and men, to repel the invasions of the northern nations. Nothing was ever so pernicious to our country, nothing was ever so unlucky … Those very people whom, when absent, they dreaded more than death itself, were invited to reside, as one may say, under the selfsame roof … They first landed on the eastern side of the island, by the invitation of the unlucky King, and there fixed their sharp talons, apparently to fight in favour of the island, but alas! more truly against it. Their mother-land, finding her first brood thus successful, sends forth a larger company of her wolfish offspring … From that time the germ of

---

5   Later of course Boudicca's reputation was restored such that today she is seen as perhaps our first ever heroine.

iniquity and the root of contention planted their poison amongst us, as we deserved, and shot forth into leaves and branches.

Worse was to come, but no more, it would seem, than we deserved:

> For the fire of vengeance, justly kindled by former crimes, spread from sea to sea, fed by the hands of our foes in the East, and did not cease, until, destroying the neighbouring towns and lands, it reached the other side of the island, and dipped its red and savage tongue in the Western ocean … Lamentable to behold, in the midst of the streets lay the tops of lofty towers, tumbled to the ground, stones of high walls, holy altars, fragments of human bodies, covered with livid clots of coagulated blood, looking as if they had been squeezed together in a press; … neither to this day are the cities of our country inhabited as before, but being forsaken and overthrown, still lie desolate …

They don't write history like that any more.

The two brothers, Hengist and Horsa, from Juteland[6] (or Jutland) having been invited by Vortigern, made Kent their own. The ensuing Angles spread up the east coast (to East Anglia), establishing themselves as the 'North Folk' (in Norfolk) and the 'South Folk' (in Suffolk). Other Angles founded the Kingdom of Mercia in Huntingdonshire and Northamptonshire. Saxons followed on in their long-boats, settling as the East Saxons (in Essex), the South Saxons (in Sussex), the Middle Saxons (in Middlesex), the Saxons of Suth Rige (in Surrey) and the West Saxons (in Wessex). The Angles it was, in their Englisc language, who first called the country Engaland (land of the Angles). (See Fig. 24.)[7]

Thus, from the ruins of Roman Kent, the descendants of Hengist and his son Oisc, father of the Oistingas, established the Kingdom of Cantware. Protected by the treacherous currents swirling around the Straits of Dover to the south, by the Thames Estuary to the north and, to the west, by Andredes Leag, a vast impenetrable forest of oak which lay, like a green sea, between the arms of the North and South Downs, the Oistingas made this corner of Britain their own, and developed their own cultural identity, distinct from the Saxons to the west and the Angles to the north.

For nearly 300 years thereafter (from 488 to 760) Kent could be regarded as a kingdom; it was certainly considered so by King Oisc (or, as he was sometimes known, Aesc) and his descendants who ruled over it. Indeed, Aesc's great grandson, King Aethelberht (more of whom anon) at one stage ruled all land south of the Humber. By the end of the eighth century, however, the last descendant of Oisc, another Aethelberht, lost his head, and Kent fell under the power of the awful Offa, King of Mercia. Mercy, as it happens, was not a commodity much employed by Offa – in point of fact, he was a major beheader. In 825 King Egbert of Wessex defeated Beornwulf of Mercia, and Kent's glory days as an independent kingdom were at an end. Lest they be forgotten, however, a record of the names of the last Kings of Kent is recorded at Appendix 3 Part 2. (See p.122.)[8]

To my mind the very best feature of these assorted teutonic raiders, and their descendants, was their names (viz, Oiscs, Aescs, Cnuts, Offas, Icels, Stufs, Egberts, Eadberts, Aethelberhts, Berthas, Eigfriths and Thingfriths). Some echo down the centuries

---

6   It is recognised that the precise origins of the Jutes is a matter of debate. Some authorities consider them to be Frisians, and other teutonic tribes who moved west to the coast from the Rhine basin. Perhaps the best explanation is that a number of different peoples took part in this mass migration to South East England (the precise composition of which we can only conjecture) and that the term 'Jute' should be regarded as a broad appellation for all of them.

7   Taken from a *Historical Atlas*, by William R. Shepherd, 1929 edition.

8   Taken from *Roman Britain and the English Settlements*, Collingwood and Myers, 1937.

to us today. Wihtgar is remembered in the Isle of Wight,[9] the Hastingas in Hastings, Wlencing in Lancing. What a pity it is then that my favourite, Wuffa (conqueror of the Eastern seaboard) has not enjoyed the same accolade. How much more interesting it would be today to live in East Wuffa than East Anglia.

Some time after the arrival of Hengist and Horsa, Jutish settlers established themselves in the Stour valley.[10] From these beginnings sprang Eggarton and Godmersham. 'Ham' is a Saxon/Jutish word for enclosed place or homestead (later, settlement) and 'ton' or 'tun' is a Saxon/Jutish word for enclosed place or farmstead. Eggarton can be translated as 'Eggar's (or Edgar's) Place'. Godmersham (in whose parish Eggarton lies) may mean Godmaere's Settlement or, as Philipott suggests, 'God's land surrounded by water'.[11] This suggests that the bend in the river, above which sits our little church of St Lawrence, was a sacred spot long before the Normans arrived. Invaders' settlements can be traced spreading down the valley, from Eggarton, to Godmersham, to Chilham, to Bagham, to Chartham – all the way to Canterbury.

The next invaders were of a different sort, seeking a different conquest. Saint Augustine and his missionaries arrived from Rome in 597 and made for Canterbury with a mission to convert the island to Christianity.[12] Here they met King Aethelbert, ruler of Kent since 560, and in 602 converted him to Christianity. Canterbury then became England's first diocese (a primacy it retains to this day) and Augustine its first archbishop;[13] the existing church building was rehallowed in 602 and dedicated to Christ Jesus the Saviour. Thus Rome with its third invasion, 500 years after the last, ultimately managed to conquer the Kingdom.

---

9   Another Jutish enclave.

10   The valleys were the first to be settled.

11   T. Philipott's *Villare Cantianum*, 1689, suggests 'Land given to God, and that church, bounded by meres'. Mere traditionally means a pond or marsh. Brade-Birks, one time Vicar of Godmersham, favours 'Godmaere's Settlement'.

12   Augustine was not the first Christian missionary to grace these shores – Aethelberht's wife was already a Christian before he ever arrived. The teachings of Christ first came to England with the Romans (along with their Pantheon of Gods) in the fourth century. Later, in the fifth century, a Briton called Patrick was captured by raiders, enslaved and taken to Ireland for six years. He then escaped to Gaul where he became a Christian. Later, in A.D. 460, he returned to Ireland as a missionary to spread the faith, set up many monasteries and died a saint. From one of these St Columba came in A.D. 563 to Iona from which he converted the Picts in Scotland. Christianity then closed in on England in a pincer movement led by St Patrick (with his Celtic brand of Christianity) from the north and St Augustine (with his Roman brand) from the south. These two strains converged on Whitby in A.D. 604 where a synod was convened to decide which was the true brand of Christianity. Roman Christianity won the day and Canterbury thus assumed a primacy over the whole of Britain which it holds to this day.

13   To this day archbishops are enshrined in the stone chair or 'Cathedra' (seat of a bishop) of St Augustine in the heart of the cathedral. The one we see today, however, is, most likely, a 13th-century copy of the seventh-century original. St Augustine went on to re-hallow the church in 602 and dedicate it to Christ Jesus the Saviour.

VIII
GOD'S LAND SURROUNDED BY WATER

There can be little doubt that the site of Godmersham church, on its bluff above a bend in the river Stour with a fine view across the valley, is a place of great antiquity. Roman bricks were found when new foundations were dug in the 19th century, and fragments of Roman pottery and Saxon material have been turned up in the graveyard. A massive yew tree, perhaps a thousand years old with a hollow trunk big enough for six men to climb into, stands sentinel in the grounds. Men and women have worshipped here and performed their rites, according to their custom, down the ages through Pagan, Roman, Saxon, and Christian times.[1]

The earliest written reference to Godmersham records Beornwulf, King of Mercia, giving 'Godmaeres Ham' (God's land surrounded or bounded by water)[2] to Wulfrid Archbishop of Canterbury, in A.D. 822[3] (although some scholars question the authenticity of this record). In any event Cwenthry, Abbess of Selemynstre in Thanet, fraudulently stole this land from him, and so Archbishop Wulfred took the matter to the Synod of Clovesho in A.D. 824, presided over by Beornwulf King of the Mercians. The Synod restored the land to him and by great good fortune a note of the bounds, or boundaries, of the estate survives, set down on the back of the record of the proceedings of the Synod.[4] It can be translated as follows:[5]

> Here is the territory of eight ploughlands in Godmersham. First from the ash, north to the ford called after Stætta's people (viz. Stettingford). Thence north along the river as far as Dreama's enclosure (Trimworth) on to the fish pool. Thence due east along to the south of the broad clearing. So on by the South part of Purr wood by the pit clearing as far as the winding valley (Winchcombe) into the muddy place. Out

---

1   Pottery dated to 500 B.C. was found in the grounds at Court Lodge.
2   For the etymology of Godmersham *see* Chapter 7 footnote 11.
3   Canterbury, DC, Reg P, fo 18 (s.xv).
4   Canterbury, DC, Reg C, fo 203 (s.xv)
5   *See* The Godmersham Project at archaeology.eu.com/godmersham, to which I am indebted for the translation by Prof. J. McN. Dodgson, of the grant found on the back of the parchment record of the Council of Clofesho of A.D. 824. The bracketed names are mine with assistance from Rev. Brade-Birks.

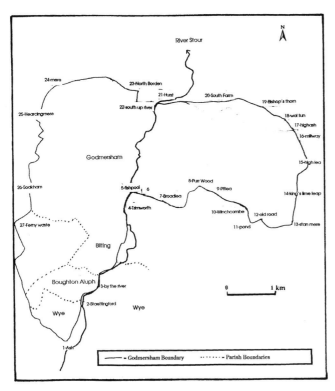

25   *Saxon bounds, A.D. 824.*

of the muddy place on to the old road. Thence into the middle of the stone pool. Thence straight on to the King's lime-heap. Away from the heap downwards across the high clearing along the 'Cross' way as far as the high ash to the North of wool farm (Waltham). So on to the Bishop's thorn. Thence west through the South farm in the middle of the wood (Middle Hurst). Thence south and upwards via the river into the Northern part of 'bord' valley. Thence into the dark pool. Out of that into the middle of the pool named after Hearca's people (Hearcincg mere). Thence to Soke valley (Soakham). So on to the fern park. So on as far as the ash.

Etymologists can have much fun marrying up this description to modern day landmarks: Purr (or 'Pure') wood, marked on today's Ordnance Survey, stands a few hundred yards away from our own house at Eggarton, its name unchanged since the ninth century. The bounds make a rectangle centred around the River Stour, with a right angle spur eastwards from Godmersham; these bounds match those of the medieval estate at the time of Domesday Book. Remarkably, they follow almost the same lines as the parish boundary of Godmersham today. Some things, it seems, never change. (*See* Fig. 25.)[6]

Some time following this grant, the land was lost to the church until, in 1037, Archbishop Egilroth bought it back from Duke Sired for '72 marcs of pure silver for the use of the monks of Christ Church (Canterbury's Cathedral Priory).'[7]

In 1067, immediately after the conquest, William I, King of England and Duke of Normandy, gave the Earldom of Kent[8] to his half brother, the powerful Bishop of Bayeux. Odo by name, odious by nature, he was a thoroughly bad lot. Godmersham narrowly missed falling prey to the odious one who took over the neighbouring estate of Chilham. Domesday Book records Chilham as having a taxable value of £30, but having to pay an extortionate £80 and 40 shillings (quadruple the amount due) in tax to Bishop Odo. He was disgraced in 1076, having defrauded the King of a number of properties. Finally he went too far and was arrested in 1082 having raised arms with the apparent intention of overthrowing the Pope.[9] Unable to try him as Bishop of Bayeux, William overcame the problem by trying him as Earl

6   As translated and transcribed by the Rev. Brade-Birks, Vicar of Godmersham, 1942.
7   Canterbury, DC, Reg C, fo 203 (s.xv). Supposedly this was to supply the convent with food and raiment. *See* T. Philipott's detailed *Villare Cantianum*, p.176.
8   Together with nearly 200 manors in his own name – one of them being Hadlow.
9   Clearly a man of some ambition, he was the only man, other than Henry VIII, who tried to take over both church and country.

of Kent and threw him into prison, passing the Earldom of Kent on to William of Ypres. King William unwisely released him on his deathbed and the odious one went on to cause more trouble for his son King William II, until his death in 1097.[10]

Godmersham, happily, remained with the monks of Christ Church throughout this time, and is recorded in Domesday Book (of 1086) as part of the lands of the Archbishop of Canterbury as follows:

> In Feleberg hundred, the Archbishop himself holds Gomersham. It was taxed at eight sulungs[11] (960 acres). The arable land is twelve carucates (1,440 acres). In demesne there are two, and sixty villeins (freemen), with eight cottagers, having seventeen carucates (1,940 acres). There is a church, and two servants (slaves), and one water-mill of twenty-five shillings, and twelve acres of meadowland. Wood for the pannage (foraging) of forty hogs. In the time of Edward the Confessor, and when he received it, it was worth twelve pounds, now twenty pounds, and yet it pays thirty pounds.

From this entry it can be seen that in Saxon/Norman times Godmersham, far from being a sleepy little hamlet, was a thriving estate of ever increasing value. Godmersham had a greater taxable acreage than the adjoining Royal Estate of Wye (eight sulungs to their seven), a more profitable mill (Godmersham's one mill, by the ford, yielding 25s. while Wye's four yielded 23s. 8d.), had more freemen than Chilham (60 villeins to their 38), and those freemen held a greater acreage (60 'ploughs' to Chilham's 38). In 1066 it had a taxable value of £12; by 1086 it was worth £20 but actually paid out £30. The monks of Christ Church, though not in the same league as Bishop Odo, clearly still knew how to extort money from their tenants. Off the back of these 'ill-gotten gains' the monks built a great manor lodge next to the church at Godmersham comprising a stone court-lodge (in 1250),[12] which the Prior himself used to frequent, a huge barn 121 feet long (in the 15th century), stables and other farm buildings.[13] The Lodge probably stood on the site of a yet earlier building – pottery fragments have been excavated in the grounds dating back to 500 B.C.

At the time of Domesday, the Abbeys of Christ Church and St Augustine's in Canterbury owned almost half of Kent, and the shadow of the Church crept over the land. Eggarton, however, managed to evade it (by a whisker) and lay outside church ownership.[14] This, in part, accounts for its colourful history. Eggarton's story is a secular one, bound up with the fate of knights and noblemen, very different from that of Godmersham whose story is entwined with that of the Church, and Wye (the Royal estate)[15] which is bound up with that of the Crown.

10   King William II would not have thanked him for this act of clemency. Following his release, Odo went on to raise a rebellion in Kent. He was captured after a six-week siege of Pevensey castle and escaped to Rochester castle, where he was captured again and finally banished from the realm.

11   A sulung was a Kentish measure of taxable land based on the area that a plough with four-pair of oxen could plough. This area roughly equates to 120 acres (depending on the terrain). It could also be referred to as one plough or one carucate.

12   Supplemented by its own chapel in 1289 and solar in 1313. Tim Tatton-Brown notes 1985.

13   Mr Charles Igglesden, Canterbury Archives ref CCA-U3-117/28/1, suggests that the Lodge was used as a summer retreat or convalescent home for the priors of Canterbury. This likely understates the importance of the lodge, since the Great Hall House was a significant manorial building which was much used by the prior – though admittedly it was not itself a priory.

14   It is interesting to guess where Eggarton's land ended and the monks' land began. I would guess this happened at the very start of Eggarton Lane – with the boundary following the route of the old Roman road. *See* map at Fig. 10, p.10.

15   Royal since Saxon times. King William I however handed over Wye to the monks of his newly created Battle Abbey, with whom it remained until the dissolution of the monasteries by King Henry VIII in 1583. Wye Court, however, was regularly visited by Medieval and Tudor kings, on their royal processions through

The 12th and 13th centuries represent the highwater mark of religion in this country and Kent found itself at the forefront of a wave of religious fervour. The Benedictines founded an abbey in Faversham in 1147, the Blackfriars (Dominicans) in Canterbury in 1221, the Whitefriars (Carmelites) in Aylesford in 1240 and the Greyfriars (Franciscans) in Canterbury in 1270. Kings, Knights and Barons, all pledged fortunes to the cause. The early wooden churches were replaced by buildings of stone, imported from Normandy, and our little church at Godmersham was rebuilt by the monks of Canterbury and dedicated to St Lawrence the Martyr; St Lawrence was roasted to death by the Emperor Valerian on a griddle in ancient Rome. His roasting is remembered in the grid on the chancel ceiling, and the villagers were no doubt grateful to him for their great annual fair each 10 August in his memory.[16]

This period of building, unparalleled since Roman times, with its churches[17] and castles,[18] changed the face of England forever. William (assisted by Archbishop Lanfranc) was as great a builder as he was a warrior, and the material he favoured was a beautiful creamy white limestone which he shipped over from his birthplace, Caen. While (a thousand years before) Caesar Augustus is supposed to have said: 'I found Rome brick and left it marble,' William might have said 'I found Britain wood, and left it stone.' The works of these early masons amaze today, but how much more impressive they must have been a thousand years ago when they soared up high and unchallenged above the surrounding landscape.

The church remained with the monks of Christ Church and, in the Kent Hundred Rolls of 1274-5,[19] instigated at the order of King Edward I, it is recorded as follows:[20]

> they also say that the Prior and the Convent of Christ Church Canterbury hold Chartham and Chilham manors from ancient times … and they say that the Prior and Convent of Christ Church have two thirds of the aforesaid hundred pertaining to their manors of Chartham and Godmersham, they do not know of what warrant.

Godmersham village (or Street as it was then known) lay a little to the north-east of the Court Lodge, up the street, by the fording of the river at the ancient seat of Ford (now Godmersham Park). With its strategic location on fertile alluvial soil by the ford, it had probably been settled since late Iron-Age times; remains of an extensive Iron-Age field system can still be seen in the Park today. Though small it was a place of some significance and highly valued by the monks of Canterbury who saw it as their 'coveted possession'.[21] In 1375 King Edward III granted Godmersham permission to hold a fair in Whitsun week and a market every Tuesday – a great concession for so small a place. No doubt being in the demesne of the grand stone court-lodge (much frequented by the Prior of Christ Church) told in its favour.[22]

---

the realm, notably Edward I and II and Henry VI and VIII. Cardinal John Kempe, Archbishop of Canterbury, King Henry VI's Chancellor and Wye's most famous son, obtained King Henry VI's blessing to building Wye College as a place of learning. Wye's *King's Head Inn* harks back to these royal connections.

16   As granted by King Edward I in 1279.

17   Notably at Canterbury, Rochester and, closer at hand, Wye.

18   Notably in Dover (with its walls 20 feet thick), Canterbury, Rochester, Chilham, Leeds and Tonbridge.

19   A Hundred was an administrative area, used for the purposes of dues and taxation, and was nominally 100 hides or sulungs. Each hundred had its own court of law. In Kent, the hundreds were part of seven (later only four) larger areas called lathes. Eggarton was in Fellborough hundred Shepway lathe.

20   At m.4.dorso Fellborough Hundred. They also took a grant of land in 1255 from Robert de la Forde.

21   T. Philipott in his *Villare Cantianum* confirms that 'in the year 1387 Thomas Arundell, Archbishop of Canterbury, with the especial licence of King Richard III appropriated the tithes of the rectory of Godmersham to the church of Christ Church to the support and maintenance of the fabric of the church aforesaid.'

22   In about A.D. 1400 Prior Chillenden divided the Court Lodge area in half keeping the inner court for

After 450 years of relatively benign rule from Canterbury, King Henry VIII came to the throne and delivered a galvanic shock through all branches of the church, dissolving the monasteries, including the Priory of Christ Church in 1540, and taking over the valuable manor lodge (with its extensive farm and other buildings) at Godmersham. This was a dark and uncertain time for the village. A few years later however, in 1546, the King returned the manor to the Dean and Chapter of Canterbury – in exchange for seven other valuable manors; a most unequal bargain but one the church had no option but to agree. There must have been rejoicing in the village. The village recovered and, in Stuart times, the market was a thriving concern. King Charles II allowed a tradesman to circulate his own token, instead of the King's coin, confidently inscribed on one side: 'Robert Oakley his half penny' and on the other 'Godmersham in Kent-The Grocer's Arms.' There was a thriving mill on the mill stream (now filled in) just below the ford. Slightly less busy, one would hope, was the ordeal pit in the river by the ford, where women felons were tried 'by ordeal'. The odds were not in their favour: if they survived they were killed for witches, and if they did not, they drowned.[23] Male criminals had a much easier time of it – they were hung on the hill at Babbele behind Little Eggarton.

By the 17th century, however, society was changing – the power of the church, though still strong in the land (and especially in Kent) was beginning to be challenged by a more confident merchant class. The monks continued to own much of the village land, but they leased out the old manor lodge and farm buildings (Court Lodge Farm) to a succession of tenants – including Richard Austen from 1669. In 1698, a stone bridge (subsequently extended) was built across the river, and inscribed:

> Built by the Parish and NOT by the County – Thomas Carter and Richard Austen SURWEIGHERS.

Relations between the church and the gentry, however, remained cordial as can be seen from the following memorial to Richard Mun, Vicar of Godmersham 1675:

> exemplary to all for his piety towards God, his loyaltie to his King, his charitie to ye poore, his faithfulness to his friend and curteous behaviour to all … he was generally beloved of all, but especially ye gentry, which his sweet carriage and learned discourse endeared to him almost beyond belief and therefore his death was ye more lamented … this monument was erected for ye preservation of his memorie which ought never to be forgotten.

This monument is strategically placed on the north side of the nave, within easy view of the pulpit – no doubt to encourage incumbents.

Later, in 1837, Edward Knight (also of the Austen family) leased the manor, and in 1850 bought it and pulled down some of these buildings.[24] Court Lodge itself, with its great hall, was finally demolished in 1955 and the old manorial lodge (other than some cellars) has now almost entirely disappeared. The great tithe barn, however, remains and its imposing size gives some idea of the former grandeur of the place.

Readers interested in the history of Godmersham church can find details below. Others more interested in the broad sweep of history should, like the pilgrims to Canterbury, hurry on by.

the priors and, from 1406, letting the outer court area and buildings as a farm. It is likely that the great barn was built at this time. T. Tatton-Brown notes of May 1985.

23 Ingelese de Hertsole was drowned in the pit, in the time of Archbishop Langton, for stealing a cloak – Sede Vacante Scrap Book III MSS Canterbury Cathedral Archives.

24 It remained in the Godmersham Park Estate until 1920, was requisitioned by the army in the Second World War and never recovered.

26   *Godmersham Church today.*

GODMERSHAM CHURCH – A POSTSCRIPT

In the Canterbury Archives, tucked in with the Register of Births, Deaths and Marriages, are the detailed notes of a survey of the church, and account of the restoration work, of 1866 by the Reverend Walter Field (the incumbent vicar at the time). These trace the development of the church through a series of sketches, reproduced over the following pages.[25]

It is not fanciful to suggest that a church, probably of wood, stood on Godmersham's bluff above the river, from the earliest Christian times. Saint Augustine carried the torch of Christianity to these shores in A.D. 597 and was instructed by Pope Gregory as follows:

> We have been giving most careful thought, to the affairs of the English and have come to the conclusion that the temples of the idols in that country should on no account be destroyed. He [Augustine] is to destroy the idols, but the temples themselves are to be aspersed with holy water, alters set up … and dedicated to the service of the true God. In this way we hope that the people … may abandon idolatry and resort to these places as before and may come to know and adore the true God.[26]

The Romans carried out this same policy (and Roman remains have been found by the churchyard) thus taking the religious tradition back to the earliest of times.

The earliest parts of the building still standing however (the north and west walls of the nave – as recorded by the Rev. Field) are probably late Anglo-Saxon. The beautiful northern apse chapel together with adjoining tower (pictured above and beside), and the hatched arch over the western door (now filled in), characterised

---

25   Though not to scale – Ref Canterbury archives CCA-U3-117/6/5/2.
26   The Venerable Bede writing between A.D. 709 and A.D. 735 detailing a letter of A.D. 601 from Pope Gregory to Bishop Augustine.

27   *Church tower and apse.*

28   *Interior of apse.*

by the creamy Caen limestone, imported by Archbishop Lanfranc following his appointment in 1070, are Early Norman.[27] Some believe that the church originally consisted simply of this tower and apse, but more likely it was designed in a cruciform style. There is today a set of five bells in the bell tower cast by Christopher Hodson, London, in 1687, together with a sixth, cast by Whitechapel Bell Foundry in 1998.[28]

The chancel was extended, probably in the 13th century, and in 1363 a chantry chapel was endowed in the south apse for the house of Eggarton, leaving the church as shown in Fig. 31.[29]

In 1730, or thereabouts, further building work took place, and two large arched bays were created on the south side, each with its own perpendicular style window and grand wooden box pew – for the great houses of Godmersham and Eggarton. These were extravagant affairs raised four foot above the floor of the nave, each accessed by its own staircase (*see* Fig. 29). Behind the staircase to the western pew, another stair led down to a large vault beneath, which in turn communicated at its south end with other vaults. A brick porch was added to the main entrance in the west end, and the south apse was pulled down – all as shown in Fig. 31.

In the second half of the 19th century the Reverend Walter Field became Vicar of Godmersham. He was an active and well-connected man, being the Secretary of the Victorian Church Restoration Committee, and he raised £1,800 for the restoration of the church which was in a very dilapidated condition. The original west door could only be reached by going down a flight of nine steps which the vicar in 1855 described as 'specially inconvenient in case of funerals … and on some occasions of heavy rain, the water has so rushed in that the church has been flooded'. The work was done with typical Victorian zeal and some of the original fabric of the building was lost. The two southern bays with their old box pews for Godmersham and Eggarton were pulled down, and a new south aisle was built. The western door with its Norman arch was filled in (part of the original Norman font, having been discovered in the old south wall, being placed in its centre), the porch

27   According to Tim Tatton-Brown. Rev. Brade-Burkes believed the apse and tower to be Saxon.
28   Just over a decade after a major restoration and rehanging of the bells in a new timber frame overseen by the appropriately named Charlie Bell and sponsored by John and Fiona Sunley the owners of Godmersham Park. The church was rededicated amidst much celebration in 1987. *See* http://kent.lovesguide.com/articles/godmersham_history.htm.
29   At some stage a south aisle may also have been built – which fell down.

PEWS SOUTH OF NAVE.

29 (Above)

pulled down and a new porch built on the south side of the southern aisle; finally the box pews (pictured below) were removed and the medieval tomb stones and tiled floor replaced by polished wooden tiles.

WEST OF NAVE.

30 (Above)

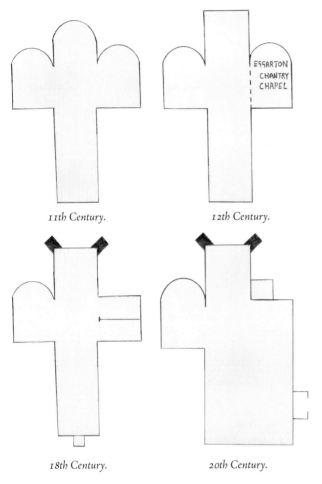

11th Century.

12th Century.

ESSARTON
CHANTRY
CHAPEL

18th Century.

20th Century.

31 *Diagrams of church development.*

One of the village boys remembers the old church as follows:[30]

The church was then in poor repair and was fitted with old deal pews so high that we could not see over the tops; the gallery was at the West end and over the altar at the East end was a table of the commandments and the belief; the aisle was paved with old tombstones and somehow we discovered that a marble thrown from the gallery with some force would make a lovely bounce and bang against the table of commandments, this of course took place before anyone came to take us through our practice; sheep were often grazed in the churchyard and with a little persuasion from us they would take very interesting leaps over the graves, this also when no one was about. I fancy I can see now the large pew at the foot of the family pew of the mansion, in which we younger children were taken to say our catechism, collects and hymns, so as to be away from the older children in the chancel where Miss Gale,[31] the Vicar's daughter, used to preside …

The rededication, on 12 August 1866, was a grand event, presided over by the Archbishop of Canterbury. The cathedral records contain a poster encouraging visitors to attend as follows:

By the obliging accommodation of the Directors of the South Eastern Railway the train that leaves Canterbury at 11.20 will stop for the convenience of persons attending the festival, opposite Godmersham Church at 11.38.

Thus the church amidst much celebration, aided by the Directors of the South Eastern Railway making a special stop at Godmersham for the first and only time, achieved the form it enjoys today.

Despite all this attention, the church today retains a quiet charm, and something remains of its former days: beneath the southern window of the chancel the observant visitor can still see some of the original medieval tiles, taken from the floor of the chancel, depicting a greyhound, a stag, a pilgrim with his staff, a fleur-de-lys, and a ghoulish figure representing death.[32] Nearby, affixed to the southern wall of the chancel, is a powerful and enigmatic bas relief of an archbishop on his seat, staring out at us across the centuries. Some believe it to be taken from the end of the original tomb of St Thomas a Becket, and to depict him, calm and immovable in the face of royal wrath, sitting beneath a

30   Charles Wills, 1856-1929. *See* further Chapter 18.
31   The children used to call the vicar old Blower Gale.
32   These are ascribed, probably wrongly, by Charles Igglesden, to the Roman period, but are more likely 14th-century.

32   *The Archbishop on his Cathedra.*

representation of Canterbury Cathedral, clad in full episcopal eucharistic robes, left hand raised in blessing, right hand grasping a serpent-headed mitre. A note in the cathedral archives[33] confidently describes this as the earliest sculpture of St Thomas, carved no later than 1200 out of Purbeck marble. How it made its journey to the Church of St Lawrence in Godmersham is not precisely known. The cathedral note suggests it came from the cathedral (perhaps smuggled out in the time of King Henry VIII when St Thomas' tomb was destroyed and his bones lost). In any event, it was hung over the porch of the prior's hall for many years,[34] greeting pilgrims as they came down the hill (following the line of the old Roman road)[35] to the priory lodge. In 1933 Lord Lewisham (then owner of the Godmersham estate) gave it to the church, and it was installed on the southern wall of the chancel upon corbels of Caen stone provided by the cathedral.

Not all historians agree that the seated figure is Thomas a Becket. Hasted, in his *History and Topographical Survey of the County of Kent*, in 1798 describes it as standing over the porch of the priory manor, 'a mansion house large and suitable to their dignity', and representing Prior Chillenden, who built a considerable part of the manorial lodge (*c.*1400).

History is not an exact science (or indeed any science at all) and we must let it retain some of its mysteries. The bas-relief remains, in short, something of an enigma – and there we must leave it.

---

33   Canterbury archives CCA-AddMs-123/20
34   Before being placed above a window at the gable end of the lodge in 1810.
35   Local legend had it that this way was so worn by the passage of pilgrim feet that no grass would ever grow upon it. Unfortunately neither the way, nor the tale, will bear close scrutiny today.

IX
A Tale of Two Cities

The great cities of Canterbury and London have, at times, viewed each other suspiciously down the length of the Pilgrim's Way. This connection between Church and State has not always been a friendly one. At times the power of one has threatened the authority of the other, none more famously than when the arrogance of King Henry II came up against the steel will of his friend Thomas a Becket, the Archbishop of Canterbury. One cold December night, in 1170, four knights[1] took leave of the King with his words, 'Who will rid me of this turbulent priest' ringing in their ears. Those knights, travelling on the trail to Canterbury, did so not with devotion but with murder in mind, and it was not long before the brains of the Archbishop were spilled over the steps of his own transept. But, as so often happens, violence produced the opposite ends to those intended. Far from subduing the power of the Archbishop and his church, the King exalted it. Henry transformed Thomas the Archbishop into Thomas the Martyr. Thomas the Martyr soon became Thomas the Saint and his tomb, in Canterbury Cathedral, became, after Rome, the most visited shrine in Christendom.

Pilgrims came in their thousands, for a blessing or a penance, to the tomb of the Saint. From all over Europe they made their way, crossing the sea to Dover or Southampton and thence to Canterbury. The word 'canter' survives to this day as a reminder of the loping gallop of pilgrims spurring their horses along the way to the tomb of the Martyr. Nor was it long before their ranks were swelled by King Henry himself, dressed in sackcloth and walking barefoot, as a penance, over the paving-slabs of the Cathedral to be scourged before his tomb; but no amount of prayers, regal or otherwise, could undo

---

1   Reginald FitzUrse, William de Tracey, Richard le Bret and Hugh de Morville.

what had been done. Just, therefore, as the Old Way was beginning to lose its place in the grand scheme of things, so it was restored by the death of a Becket at the whim of a king.

The Archbishop lost his battle but won the war. The power of the Church waxed over the land for three more centuries until, faced with another Henry, the poles of Church and State again crossed with disastrous results. King Henry VIII infuriated by the refusal of the Church to connive in his matrimonial manoeuvrings and jealous of its wealth, sought to break its power and confiscate its riches. In 1536 he ordered the dissolution of the monasteries. Never before had a monarch's decision brought such devastation to the fabric of the country. At a stroke, the string of palaces and abbeys, with their attendant manors and farms, all along the way from London to Canterbury were brought down. Like beads off a broken necklace they fell to the ground and were smashed: Otford, Wrotham, Boxley, Hollingborne, Lenham, Charing and, the end of the line, St Augustine's in Canterbury. St Thomas himself, lying in his Cathedral, was finally done down – shrine overthrown and bones carried away.[2] Even our own little church of St Lawrence in Godmersham was not immune from the storm which raged over the land. It too was taken by the King but, in a last minute reprieve, given back to the Dean and Chapter of Canterbury, in exchange for seven other manors – an unequal bargain but one they were in no position to refuse.

Hilaire Belloc, with his deep feeling for the English countryside, felt this loss, and the diminution of the Old Road, deeply: 'I know of no district in England where the heavy, gross and tortured face of Henry in his decline haunts us more. Sacredness is twofold – of pleasure and of pain – and this, the sacred end of our oldest travel, suffered in proportion to its sanctity.'

Pilgrims became a rarer sight upon the trail. The bones of the Saint, their object of veneration, were no more. The Old Road fell into disuse. The ridges were abandoned for the plains. Straight roads and turnpikes sprang up in the valleys. Men travelled in carriages. Canals became the arteries of communication, then railways. The old ways faded until, in the 20th century, the Old Road entered its last phase.

In its earliest incarnation it was the first of roads, bringing men west, across the land-bridge, from Europe after the last Ice Age. They travelled across the Downs to the heart of the country at Stonehenge. From the start it had a double significance, physical and spiritual, to those who travelled upon it. It was more than a track, it was a journey.

Then the old ways passed, new ways grew up, and the Old Road entered its second incarnation, as a pilgrim trail. Pilgrims now travelled east to Canterbury, in hope or despair, looking for a blessing or a penance. But after King Henry VIII aimed his dagger at the heart of the Church, the pilgrims fell away and we entered a more secular age. The Old Road atop the Downs began to fade, out of sight and mind; but before it was quite forgotten, it was restored, and trod once more, not by pilgrims, but yet by men with a sense of history; men like Belloc, who knew where it had come from, where it went to and what it meant.[3] So now it has entered its third incarnation, as a trail for those in search of recreation or something more.

---

2   Though local legend has it that they were secreted away, before the King's men arrived, and lie still, in a hidden resting place, within the Cathedral.

3   There is a wonderful depiction of such a man's love for the Old Road in Michael Powell and Emeric Pressburger's film *A Canterbury Tale*, set in the Stour valley. It was filmed during the Second World War to boost the morale of our troops through its portrayal of the Downland countryside and its village folk.

Today it is possible once more to walk from Winchester to Canterbury, following our ancestral memories along the crest of the Downs, enjoying, like those who went before, the same rolling whale-backed Downs beneath the same limitless sky.

33 *Canterbury Cathedral.*

X

WILLIAM DE VALENCE

Eggarton is not recorded in Domesday Book. It is first mentioned later in connection with the estate of Aymer de Valence, Earl of Pembroke, who held the Manor of Eggarton at his death in the 17th year of the reign of King Edward II – 1324.[1] It is surmised that he was either given Eggarton by the King or inherited it from his father William de Valence, the 1st Earl of Pembroke (1225-96) to whom we now turn.

William de Valence, of the ancient house of Lusignan, was an Angevin knight, related to the Plantagenet Kings of England.[2] His mother was a famous beauty, Isabella of Angouleme, the widow of King John, King of England, 1199-1216, and mother of King Henry III. His father was Hugh of Lusignan – whom Isabella married after the death of John. William was thus half brother to King Henry III and uncle to King Edward I (*see* the Valence family tree, p.52). In the incessant struggle to establish the balance of power between the King and the Barons in the 14th century he was a weighty supporter of the Royal House of Plantagenet. It is possible that William acquired the manor of Eggarton in the course of his eventful life (indeed he may have won and lost it on more than one occasion).

William was a warrior in the best tradition of the House of Plantagenet – that most militant of dynasties, which could boast such as Henry II, Edward I (the Hammer of the Scots), Richard the Lion Heart and Henry V. Indeed the Plantagenets pursued perhaps the longest of all wars, the Hundred Years War, against the House of Vallois in France, before they turned in upon themselves in the War of the Roses.

William was born in Valence, south-east of Lusignan, south of Poitiers (part of the province of Poitou in the west central part of France) in 1225. When the Capetin French conquered Poitou in 1247, King Henry III invited William to England. He quickly became a royal favourite and Henry granted him many important positions and properties including castles at Goodrich, Pembroke, Hereford and Hartford. William had an eye for property

---

1   *The History and Topographical Survey of the County of Kent*, Volume 7, 1724, by Edward Hasted.
2   Founded by King Henry II, son of Geoffrey of Anjou and the Empress Matilda, the House of Plantagenet, or first House of Anjou, was so named for the sprig of broom, 'plante de genet', which Geoffrey wore in his helmet.

and married an heiress, Joan de Munchise (or Munchensey). Through her he became the 1st Earl of Pembroke,[3] Lord of Wexford in Ireland, and Lord of Swanscombe in Kent. This is the first connection to be found between the Lords of Valence and the County of Kent.[4]

In Norman times a king did not rule by divine right but by his own force of character and on the sufferance of his knights. The balance of power would ebb and flow between them. As a half brother to the King, and one who enjoyed the royal largesse, William was very much in the royal camp. He therefore became an enemy of the Barons – and in particular Simon de Montfort.

This, however, did not concern William. He was bred and trained as a knight, with all the martial skills that went with that, and there was nothing William liked more than a good fight. He could normally find one somewhere. If things became too quiet in France, there was always England, or, if all else failed, the Saracens in the Holy Lands. William managed to spend most of his time at war or in the saddle riding from one campaign to the next. In the course of his eventful life, he was exiled once from France to England, three times from England to France, spent 17 years fighting the Welsh (with an occasional foray into Scotland for good measure), went on two crusades to the Holy Lands, and occupied the rest of his time at war with the Barons. In fact he was so busy fighting that he never had time to be formally invested as the Earl of Pembroke though this did not prevent him from going to Parliament under that name in 1295. In between campaigns he found time to marry Joan de Munchise, Lady of Swanscombe and Countess of Pembroke, in 1247, and to father five children. The principal events in his life are set out on the timeline on p.51.

William was a man of immense energy and his business was war. As a knight of the realm, that was what he trained for and that was what he did. It may seem strange that he was able fight so many battles without being killed (especially as he was occasionally on the losing

---

3   Slightly confusingly, although William seems to be known as the 1st Earl of Pembroke, there were in fact earlier Marshal Earls of Pembroke (nine of them), the most famous of whom was William de Marshal, 1st Earl of Pembroke (died 1219), a Knight Templar, who has a magnificent tomb-stone carved in his likeness in Temple Church London. Marshal by name martial by nature, he was Earl Marshal of England for King Henry III. He was also Joan de Munchensey's (William's wife's) grandfather. It was through his wife that William gained his title. It seems, however, that neither William nor Aymer was ever formally invested, but their Earldom tacitly assumed. This may have been because William's wife, Joan, had an older sister, the Countess of Norfolk, who also had a claim to the Earldom. When the Ninth and last Marshal Earl died without male heir the Earldom would usually have passed to the eldest sister and through her to her husband; however, an ancient Norman tradition laid down that an Earldom was an interest which went with the land (all Norman Earls, as equal peers, holding their land from the King). Thus when Pembroke castle and estate went to Joan, the younger sister, as her share of the Marshal estates, the right to the Earldom came into question. The King may have been reticent in conferring the Earldom on one of his French family from overseas in the face of a rival claim from an established English family. The Countess of Norfolk, however, never claimed the title and it was tacitly assumed that William acquired that honour. He attended the early 'parliament' as such, but it was not until the end of his life that William was referred to as Earl of Pembroke in official documents.
4   By early 1252 Henry III had begun to find William additional manors, which could have included Eggarton (See Oxford Dictionary of National Biography, Volume 56, under William de Valence). We know that in 1256 Henry gave him the nearby manor of Sutton, renamed Sutton Valence after him, and that in 1267, after helping King Henry III defeat the Barons at the Battle of Evesham, he was rewarded with further lands by the King in South East England, and that he died in Brabourne Manor just a few miles south-east of Eggarton. The first recorded mention of Eggarton however is made in connection with his son Aymer. It is not clear, however, whether Aymer inherited Eggarton from his father or acquired it himself. Eggarton, however, does not appear to have been recorded as part of William's estate when he died (see Inquisition Post Mortem, 24 May 1296) but this is not decisive, since Brabourne Manor is not recorded either (and this was certainly his). It remains possible, therefore, that Eggarton was amongst William's own holdings in Kent. William may well have found Eggarton a useful base in Kent since the nearby Royal Manor of Wye was regularly visited by Kings Edward I and II and their courts.

side). His survival though tells us something about the rules of chivalry according to which knights lived their lives. If a knight was captured in battle he was more likely to lose his fortune, by way of ransom, than his life, and more likely to be exiled than put to the sword. William was exiled on a number of occasions.

William's life was shaped by the ebb and flow of power between the King and Barons. He found it very convenient to have a foot on both sides of the Channel. Having lost his estate in Poitou to the Capetin French he established a new estate in England. He then lost his lands in England and was exiled to Poitou once more in 1258. Two years later he returned to England and recommenced battle with the Barons – at the siege of Northampton. Three years after this, the tide again turned; De Montfort got the upper hand at the Battle of Lewes and William had to return to his home from home in France. After being reconciled with Simon de Montfort, he returned to England, but fought for the King against the Barons in the Battle of Lewes. When the Barons won the day he again fled to France before finally returning in 1265 and helping the King to victory over the Barons at the Battle of Evesham. After this, his estates were restored and his fortunes more secure.

Medieval warfare was a bloody affair, but it was conducted by rules of behaviour more civilised than our own. It has taken a thousand years, and the drafting of the Geneva Convention, before we can claim anything to compare with the ancient laws of chivalry. The 14th century was a time of almost continuous war for the nobility (as indeed it had been for centuries before). The owner of Eggarton would have been a largely absentee landlord, spending his time fighting for his King in distant lands. Indeed the lands of Eggarton may have been won and lost on more than one occasion, as its lord's fortunes ebbed and flowed. Today, with the ownership of land more widespread than before, a landlord is simply the absentee owner of a property, who lets another occupy it in return for a rent. In medieval times, with land concentrated in the hands of the nobility, a landlord would literally be the lord of the land, to whom feudal dues were owed, and who in turn owed allegiance to the King.

William died, as he would probably have chosen, fighting. His death, like his life, was an affair of two countries. In 1296 he was wounded in a skirmish in France and was carried bleeding back to England. He got as far as his Manor at Brabourne in Kent, six miles south of Eggarton, before finally giving out; who knows, perhaps he was even heading home to Eggarton to die. William was buried in Westminster Abbey near the tomb of Henry III, his half brother and his King whom he served so well.[5] This was a signal honour for one outside the direct line of monarchy. King Henry's body lies in a tomb of Purbeck marble, inlaid with porphyry and glass, at the heart of the Abbey that he spent much of his life rebuilding,[6] his heart, however, was taken to the Abbey of Fontevrault in France, to lie with his Angevin forefathers. William de Valence's body (complete) rests in his tomb, in the Chapel of St Edmund and Thomas the Martyr, to the south of the high altar (*see* p.59).[7] He lies beneath a wooden effigy of himself in full armour (naturally) with his feet on a lion – as befits one who went on crusade. His tomb, like his life and his death, is an affair of two countries – it has a heart of English oak, and a surface (originally) of French fancy. It was formerly covered in copper gilt and limoge enamel (the latest fashion

---

5   It is believed that he was originally entombed by the tomb stone in the floor by the high altar near the tomb of Henry III and moved at some later date to the Chapel of St Edmund and Thomas the Martyr to the south of the high altar – where his tomb stands today.

6   Henry III's tomb is just to the north of the high altar (and adjacent to the tomb of Edward the Confessor which lies behind the altar).

7   On the right as you enter.

from France), and would have shone like the sun as the morning light penetrated the southern windows, dazzling any English onlookers with its splendour. Sadly little of this embellishment remains today, having been ransacked, in all likelihood, at the time of the Reformation. It still remains, however, an important tomb and one of the earliest examples of a 'tomb of kinship' in England.[8]

I visited the Abbey one day in search of the Valence tombs and asked one of the wardens if he knew anything of them. Together we looked at the cathedral reference book on its tombs and memorials and discovered where they lay.

The warden then directed me through the cloisters to the chapter house. Next to this is a stout oak door with a sign and entry-phone beside marked Keeper of the Library and Muniments. I rang the bell, explained my interest to the voice coming down the line and was surprised to be invited in. Pushing open the door and ascending the flight of stairs behind, I found myself in the abbey library, deserted (not being open to the public) and lined with its collection of 16,000 valuable leather-bound books and manuscripts. In one corner of the library was a circular wooden staircase which led me up to the muniment room housing the abbey archives. Here the Keeper of the Muniments met me and found me some texts; for a while, as I pored over these books high above the cloister, I was transported back to the medieval times of the tombs (and their occupants).

We may never know whether or not William de Valence owned Eggarton, though he certainly owned estates round about. What we do know, however, is that the first written reference to Eggarton is made in connection with William's son Aymer, and to him we now turn.

WILLIAM DE VALENCE TIMELINE

1225	Born in Valence, South of Poitiers
1247	Loses land in France and comes to England
1249	Marries Joan de Munchise. Becomes Earl of Pembroke
1249	Appointed join Ambassador to France
1249-50	Goes on crusade with King Henry III to Holy Lands
1253-4	Goes with King Henry to Acquitane
1255	Fights beside King Henry in North England
1258	Falls out with de Montfort, is captured and exiled to France
1261	Returns to England. Fights for King against Barons at Northampton
1264	Is defeated be De Montfort at Battle of Lewes. Escapes to France.
1265	Returns and helps King defeat Barons at Battle of Evesham
1266	Besieges Bury St Edmunds
1270-2	Goes of Crusades to Palestine
1273	Returns to France
1277-94	Returns to his seat in Pembroke and fights Welsh
–	Ambassador to Scotland
1295	Comes to Parliament
1296	Wounded whilst in France. Returns home to die in Braburne Manor, Kent. Buried near King Henry III in the St Edmund Chapel, Westminster Abbey

---

8   *See Gothic Tombs of Kinship*, by Anne McGee Morganstern (p.64), a copy of which scholarly work I was kindly allowed to read by the Keeper of the Muniments at Westminster Abbey.

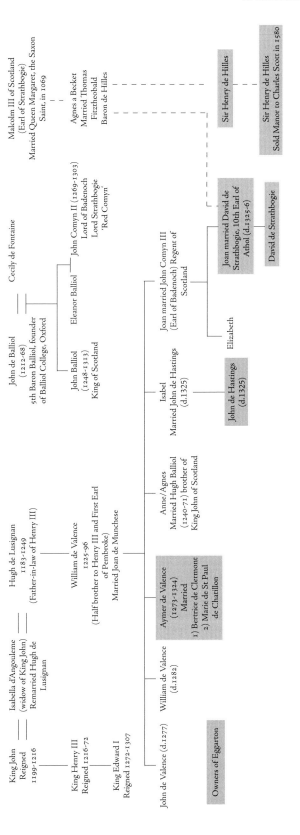

34 *Valence family tree.*

35 *Valence family shield.*

XI

AYMER DE VALENCE

William de Valence had four daughters and three sons – the youngest being Aymer (*see* Valence family tree, p.52) Aymer was born in 1273 or 1275 (differing sources offer different dates) and died, suddenly, in 1324. Though some doubt surrounds his dates of birth and death, there is no doubt that he was one of the foremost knights of his time, taking precedence, ultimately, over all other barons in the land.

Aymer is recorded as owning Eggarton at the time of his death.[1] Eggarton in the course of its history has a knack of being involved with great figures of the day and Aymer de Valence is no exception. Like his father he made his way in the world by force of arms, building his reputation, and fortune, in the chivalric tournaments held by King Edward I in France. Described as 'tall and pale' by the acerbic Piers de Gaveston, he was a man of considerable strength and stature (though not quite able to match the six foot two inches of Edward Longshanks). It was possible to amass considerable sums by taking prisoner other knights in the foray, and releasing them in return for ransom. Though this may appear much like hostage-taking today, it was standard practice amongst the knights of the day, forming part of their code of chivalry, and serving to train and equip them for battle in the service of their King. On one occasion, Aymer was the victor in one of these forays and, on search being made for him to give him his prize, was found with his head on the anvil of the local blacksmith; the smith was busy bashing Aymer's helmet which had become so dented and misshapen in the battle he was unable to remove it.

It seems, however, that Aymer may have had another side to him. He was described, in a petition to the Pope (requesting to be given 'a plurality of benefits') as 'a youth of good ability recommended by his study of letters and his manner and merits'. This would not be the first time (or the last) that a written reference had been a little liberal with the truth. Suffice it to say, that he is remembered less for his scholarship than his

---

1 See *The History and Topographical Survey of the County of Kent*, by Edward Hasted, Second edition, Volume 7, pp.325-7. *See also*: Ancestry.com under 'Lusignan' (106516.2301@compuserve.com).

36 *Aymer de Valence's estates in England.*

feats of arms.[2] What is not in doubt, as will be seen, is that he was a man of principle, for whom the rules of chivalry provided the moral compass of his life.

In his early years Aymer had to make his way through such deeds of daring since, with two elder brothers standing between him and inheritance, he had little prospect

---

2   J.R.S. Phillips, the foremost expert on Aymer de Valence, however, in his book, *Aymer de Valence Earl of Pembroke 1307-1327*, depicts him as a man caught up in the politics of his time who did his best to steer a middle way between the rebellious Barons with their grievances against the King (with which Aymer may secretly have had some sympathy) and the weak easily-led monarch (with whom his natural and familial loyalty lay).

of taking over his father's fortune. His eldest brother John, however, died in 1277 and his next brother William was killed in battle in Wales in 1282. On his father's death in 1296, therefore, Aymer inherited his lands in Calais and Poitou,[3] including Rancon, Bellac and Champagnac north of Limoges, and Montignac, near Angouleme. He next inherited his mother's lands in England, and became Earl of Pembroke, on her death in 1307. Through inheritance, conquest and marriage he became the owner of great tracts of land stretching from Gloucester to East Anglia in England, as well as Wexford in Ireland, Poitou and Calais in France, Pembrokeshire, on the Welsh border, and parts of Kent including Eggarton. Thus did the Dukes of Valence share in the Angevin Empire, the greatest seen in Western Europe since the time of the Romans, stretching from the highlands of Scotland in the north, to the snow capped peaks of the Pyrenees in the south.[4] [5]

Aymer, like his father, fought many campaigns and was caught up in the great struggle for power between the King and the Barons. A timeline showing the principal events in his life is set out overleaf.

Aymer's dealings with the monarchy were more complicated than his father's. Bound by ties of kinship, he was a supporter of his cousin King Edward I, or Edward Longshanks as he was known (by reason of his long arms and legs). It would have been easy for Aymer to swear fealty to such a King. Edward was a giant among men and a fierce warrior. First, with the help of Aymer's father, he subjugated the Welsh, encircling them with a chain of castles, overlooked by the Earls of Valence from their strong-hold in Pembroke. Next he turned his attention to Scotland, determined that the Scots in turn be ruled from Westminster. In a bloody campaign he invaded the country and, taking the touchstone of Scottish Kings, the Stone of Scone (or Stone of Destiny), brought it back to Westminster.[6] There he placed it under the coronation throne of the Kings of England in Westminster Abbey. There it remained for 700 years. The Scots remained defiant, however, so in the year 1300 (three years after the death of William de Valence), Edward sent young Aymer, his cousin, to be his military commander in Scotland. Aymer fought a long campaign, defeating Robert the Bruce in 1306 at the battle of Methven, gaining some revenge on the man who had widowed his sister Joan by killing her husband, John Comyn. In part, Edward Longshanks owed his fearsome reputation as a soldier, and his successes in Wales and Scotland, to the Dukes of Valence: Aymer and his father William.

Like his father, Aymer was an energetic man and managed, meanwhile, to fit in embassies to France in 1301, 1303 and 1307.[7] The year 1307, however, proved to be a turning point. In that year King Edward I died and was buried in Westminster Abbey near the High Altar. His tomb is of plain marble with no effigy (it is thought that his coffers were exhausted by the time of his death) yet it has a sombre stateliness to it, in keeping with the dour nature of the man. Perhaps, after all, it was what he wanted. The old King may have gone but his implacable anger against the Scots lived on. On one side of his tomb were inscribed the words: 'Here lies Edward, hammer of the Scots'.

3   The province in central West France whose capital is Poitiers.
4   At its height at the start of the reign of King Henry III.
5   Fig. 36, as mapped by J.R.S. Phillips, shows his estates in England and Wales.
6   Though some believe that the Scots had hidden the real stone, and that Edward I brought back a substitute.
7   Altogether he is recorded as visiting France a total of 17 times.

AYMER DE VALENCE TIMELINE

1273 or 1275	Born
1295	Marries Beatrice de Clermont
1297	Fights for King Edward I in Flanders
1300-7	Commands King's army in Scotland
1301-3	Ambassador to France
1307	Edward II comes to throne. Aymer joins Barons as a Lord Ordainer
1308	Captures Piers de Gaveston (Earl of Cornwall) – King's favourite
1308	Sides with King after untimely death of Gaveston
1308-9	Ambassador to the Pope in Avignon
1312	Ambassador to France
1312	Ambassador to Pope in Avignon. Given New Temple and London land
1314	King's Lietenant in Scotland
1317	Saves King at Bannockburn
1317	Embassy to Pope in Avignon. Captured and ransomed
1318	Restores Edward to power over Barons
1322	Defeats Barons in Civil War at Boroughbridge. Remarries Marie de St Pol
1323	Regains New Temple and Earl of Lancaster's estates
1324	Dies in Picardy on Embassy for King

On the other was a short direct message to his son: 'Keep troth'! So worried indeed was he that his son might go soft on the Scots that he left orders for his bones to be boiled away from his body and carried into battle with the English army – continuing his campaign against the Scots from beyond the grave. Edward II, having sent his father's body (whole) back to Westminster, was soundly beaten by the Bruce at Bannockburn. Aymer indeed had to lead him from the field to avoid capture. His father's worst fears were confirmed.

It was not difficult to keep troth with the old King. He was a horseman, a falconer, a soldier – everything a medieval knight should be. The new King, Edward II, however, was not a martial man (quite the opposite in fact) and not someone the Duke of Valence was likely to respect. Faced with the King's scandalous conduct with the notorious libertine Piers Gaveston, Aymer turned away and sided with the Barons. This was not an easy decision for one whose instincts and blood ties were with the monarchy. The King, by his conduct, had forfeited allegiance, and Aymer became one of the 42 Lords Ordainers who curtailed his power. Piers Gaveston, his favourite, was banished to France.

Aymer would not have had to look far back in his own family history to find that France, a short hop over the channel, was not the ideal place to banish a person. Piers Gaveston found his way back to England the following year. Aymer, as always at the front of any queue when there was fighting to be done, besieged him at Scarborough Castle and persuaded him to give himself up in return for a promise of safekeeping.

The fighting having ceased, Aymer took himself off to visit his wife. In his absence, the other Barons took the opportunity to visit de Gaveston, whereupon he met his terrible end (in every sense of the word). On discovering what had happened, Aymer was furious. Though no friend of de Gaveston, he saw this as a breach of the chivalric code by which he lived his life, and an impeachment of his honour. In the face of this outrage, he felt he had no option but to forswear the Baron's cause, and transfer his allegiance to the King. Aymer, as has been seen, was a useful person to have on your side when there was fighting to be done and, with his support, the balance of power tilted back in the King's favour. It proved a turning point and thereafter the Barons were increasingly marginalised. Thus was the struggle between King and Barons decided – on the honour of the Duke of Valence.

This vignette tells us much about Aymer, the knight, and the rules by which he led his life. Struggles for power today take place in the Houses of Parliament – the balance having tilted irreversibly away from the Monarch in favour of the Lords and elected representative of the Commons. It is impossible now to imagine politicians being prepared to stand or fall, live or die, for the sake of their word.

Aymer became increasingly important to the King. He became his Lieutenant in Scotland in 1314 and saved the King's life at the battle of Bannockburn in 1317 – when the Scots exacted their revenge on the English. Later that year he went on an Embassy to the Pope in Avignon, in the course of which he was captured, imprisoned by Count Edouard of Bar, and ransomed for £10,400.[8] This was a fortune in those days, a veritable King's ransom, and left Aymer financially embarrassed for the rest of his days.

Later, when the King's outrages again stirred the Barons (led by the Earl of Lancaster) to civil war, Aymer defeated them at the Battle of Boroughbridge and was rewarded by the King with much of Lancaster's lands. He clearly became indispensible to King Edward and was appointed 'Keeper of the Realm' in 1320 while Edward was in Aquitaine. His first wife, Beatrice de Cleremont, then died, and in 1321 or 1322 he took a younger second wife, Marie de St Paul de Chatillon, the daughter of Guy de Chatillon (Count of St Paul and Butler of France) and great grand-daughter of King Henry III, further cementing his ties with the French aristocracy and English Monarchy.[9] Marie was aged 18 at the time of her marriage and legend has it that she was maiden, wife and widow all on the same day – when Aymer died in a joust on his wedding day. Though such an end would have been entirely fitting for a knight such as Aymer, alas the facts, here, get in the way of a good story. More reliable records show that he died (possibly poisoned) three years later on an embassy in Picardy. Like his father before him, he met his end in France and was brought back to be buried in Westminster Abbey, near the Kings he had served – an honour reserved for the leading knights of the realm.

Aymer might have died and been buried in slightly straightened circumstances,[10] but the young wife he left behind, 21-year-old Marie de St Paul, was very much alive and she was determined he should be well remembered. She managed to get him the best available spot left in the Abbey to the left of the high altar (being the first tomb you

8   Aymer's illegitimate son Henry was imprisoned with him. An initial payment of £2,500 was made (funded by the King who needed him back) which secured Aymer's release. He swore an oath to pay the balance and his son Henry and six retainers were retained as hostages. He had trouble raising the necessary funds, however, and one, Constantine de Mortimer, was still captive at his death in 1324.

9   It is interesting to note how Aymer, in his personal life, twice chose to marry important members of the French aristocracy (unlike his father who married an English heiress). He was more Angevin than Anglo-Saxon. These links with France, however, proved very valuable and ensured that whenever there was an important diplomatic mission needed overseas, Edward chose Aymer, with his French connections, to lead them. Marie brought with her land in the Pas de Calais.

10   He was not on the breadline however, enjoying an annual income of £3,000 at his death – *see Aymer de Valence, Earl of Pembroke*, by J.S.R. Phillips.

come to, straight ahead as you enter the north door). The tomb is one of the finest in the Abbey eclipsing, rather undiplomatically, even that of King Edward I; perhaps as his great grand-daughter she thought she could get away with this bit of family cheek.[11] There is a fine effigy of Aymer lying on top of the tomb, his feet on a lion, conveying something of the size of the man. Aymer is shown on horseback above the tomb in the richly carved canopy, at the top of which his soul appears fluttering up to heaven.

---

11   Get away with it she did, though the little statue of herself, second from the right of the family statues lining the north side of the casket, lost its head later on in the Reformation.

38   *William de Valence's tomb in Westminster.*

The Valences take up more than their fair share of the Abbey. Aymer's brother John de Valence (died 1277) and his sister Margaret de Valence (died 1276), both of whom died while they were only children, are buried near the altar in the shrine of the Confessor, beneath a gravestone inlaid with some of the famous Cosmati mosaic. Marie herself has a memorial tablet nearby on the wall of the north ambulatory.[12] They are perhaps the best represented family outside the monarchy in the Abbey.

Marie remained faithful, for a further 50 years, to the memory of a husband she had known but two. She was an industrious lady founding an Abbey, Denny Abbey in Cambridgeshire, to the memory of her husband;[13] not content with this, Marie went on to found a college in Cambridge – Pembroke College, which survives to this day. It was the third Cambridge college to be constituted and was initially known as the Hall of Valence Mary. Aymer, had he lived to see the college, may have supported the preference given to French students which its statutes required. He is unlikely to be so enthusiastic about the requirement (emanating from his wife no doubt) that students should report any fellow student found indulging in excessive drinking or visiting houses of disrepute. Given that the college was intended to commemorate the Earl, his wife made no attempt (so far as we know) to include a statute forbidding fighting.

Rather surprisingly, Aymer died without any legitimate heir[14] and his manor at Eggarton then passed down in accordance with the medieval laws of testament. In 1323, just prior to his death, he is recorded as having owned Eggarton Manor and as giving another property in Kent, Milton, to the church. Whether he inherited Eggarton from his

---

12   Marie de St Pol, Countess of Pembroke, 1304-77. She also founded a chantry in his memory – now part of the Chapel of St John.
13   Where she herself is buried.
14   Though it seems he had an illegitimate one.

father or acquired it himself, we cannot be certain. Neither can we know whether Aymer actually stayed there or not, but I like to think that he looked in on his Manor on his way as ambassador to Picardy or Avignon; or perhaps his father, on his way to or from one of his frequent exiles, came clanking up the lane in his armour, and stabled his horse in our house. Some trace at any event has been left by the Earls of Valence on the map of Kent. A nearby town, Sutton Valence, harks back to them[15] and the neighbouring house, up the lane to the north, to this day, is called Valence Dene.[16] [17] [18]

---

15   King Henry III gave William de Valence the manor of Sutton in 1256, and from him the village takes its name.

16   A search of the National Archives for 'Eggarton' does in fact reveal one earlier reference to Eggarton as follows: 'John de Glaseleye and Hugh his son, Clerk, Sun, the eve of All Saints, 5 Edw. I John has granted to Hugh, for a certain sum of money, all his land in the vill of Eggarton, to hold of the chief lord of the fee at 12d. a year to the court at Wethulle. Endorsed Salops Stottesdon. Witnesses: Richard Lord of Aston Boterel, Walter de Norton, Richard son of Richard de Ingwardyn, Richard son of Roger of the same, John son of Odo de Wethulle. – At Eggarton'. This record is held at Berkeley Castle. I believe, however, that this is an unrelated Eggarton though I have not been able to gain further information about this.

17   Possibly some trace of the Earls of Valence has also been left on the population of Kent, one Aymer Valence being found living in Faversham according to the 1901 census.

18   A dene or denehole is a medieval chalk mine. Farmers would dig them near fields in order to obtain high grade chalk from the deeper levels of the downs, to spread on their fields as a top dressing and to improve drainage. These deneholes were usually three to six feet in diameter and up to 40 feet deep. Underground the excavations continued in a number of chambers – up to six radiating out from the central borehole. In medieval times deneholes and wells dotted the Kent countryside. Most of these deneholes have now been covered over or naturally filled in.

XII

A TALE OF TWO VILLAGES

Crundale – Brabourne

A short walk down the valley, south east from Eggarton, takes you to the neighbouring parish, and village, of Crundale – the dale under a high crowned hill.[1] We know, from the register of Leeds Abbey (in Kent), that its early name was Dromwaed. By the time Henry II came to the throne it was known as Dromwide. Edward Hasted, that tireless chronicler of 18th-century Kent, described Crundale as follows:

It is but a small parish, containing within it not more than twenty-four houses; it is an out of the way situation, having little or no traffic through it. The hills are very frequent in it, and exceedingly barren; the soil is in general chalk, covered with quantities of flints. The country here is very healthy; it is exceeding cold, and has a wild and dreary appearance, great part of it consists of open downs, most of which are uncultivated, those on the eastern side lying on the high ridge of hills adjoining to Wye downs.[2]

From the ridge above Eggarton is a clear sight line to the spire of Crundale church, dedicated to St Mary the Blessed Virgin. It is carefully placed on a high knoll serving as a beacon for pilgrims on the way to Canterbury, but curiously remote from the living village. It is a charmed place, set within a circle of yew trees with paths radiating out from it in all directions. This ancient circle suggests a past far older than its Norman walls. Its listing in the Domesday Monachorum[3] as one of eight subsidiary churches to Wye's 'head church' suggests it may have been founded in the seventh or eighth century, after Saint Augustine's arrival at Canterbury. Roman foundations have been found in the churchyard.

---

1   According to Philipott's *Villare Cantianum*, 1689. An alternative explanation is that it derives from the old English 'Crun', meaning chalk, and 'dala' meaning dell or valley.
2   Parishes: Crundal, *The History and Topographical Survey of the County of Kent*, Volume 7 (1798), pp.368-81.
3   The Domesday Monachorum of Canterbury Cathedral is a text, compiled at the same time as Domesday Book, showing the estates of the Archbishop of Canterbury and the Monks of Christchurch. Wye's listing as a 'head church' may indicate it was one of the early 'Minster Churches', administering to its eight satellites listed as: Ashford, Eastwell, Brook, Crundale, Trimworth, Hinxhill, Brixiestun, and Hawkhurst. *See* A. Everitt, *A Continuity and Colonisation: The Evolution of Kentish Settlement*.

The flint knapping on the north and south walls of the church is as fine a work as you could hope to see anywhere in the country, the flints set so close together that they need scarcely any mortar. They are as sturdy today as when they were laid eight centuries ago by Roger de Crundale – a court mason who retired to Crundale in 1297-8.

On a tomb by the door is a laughing priest – the Reverend John Sprot, much loved Rector of Crundale 1431-66. On the wall in the nave is a picture of a white unicorn, a lion rampant and the initials A.R. – the royal coat of arms of Queen Anne (signifying the union of England and Scotland). Above the pulpit is a mysterious black Madonna (carved by L. Cubit Bevis in 1964).

This quiet spot, aloof yet welcoming, encircled by the dead beneath their stones, inspired the following lines:

40 *The laughing priest.*

> Here rest the dead upon a lonely hill
> In solitude remote – the old grey church
> Guards still her children in their last long sleep.
> The shadows of the Beech trees and the Yews
> Cast sombre twilight on the stillness round.
> Beyond these shadows in the evening light
> Gold still lingers on the Harvest fields.
> Blue mist over the distant village steals.
> The narrow lane curves down and winds away
> Past farm and cottage homes and leaves the church
> A lonely figure, standing on the hill
> Guarding her children in their long sleep.[4]

On the banks of the river Stour, two miles south west of Eggarton is the Manor of Tremworth, which in ancient times embraced the parish of Crundale, but later declined and was subsumed within it. According to Hasted, the Valoigns family possessed the manors of Tremworth and Vanne,[5] in the time of King Stephen (1135-54). Allen de Valoignes then resided at Tremworth in the reign of King Henry II (1154-89). William de Valoignes added Ashford to his estate in 1236. Waretius de Valoignes (sometimes known as Valoynes) went on Crusade with King Henry III to Palestine and was rewarded with further estates in Kent. When King Edward I called for two knights to be sent from each county for counsel, to 'parler' with the King in what some would say was the first Parliament, it was Waretius de Valoigns, along with Richard de Scoland, who was called upon to represent Kent.

Later, during the reign of Edward II, he acquired the estates of Crundale and Hadloe from John de Handlou.[6] The Valoigns family also owned the manors of Forde and Yallande in the parish of Godmersham,[7] which eventually were passed down to the Austen family,

---

4   Margaret Sage.
5   Crundale is mentioned in Domesday Book as having a manor called Fanne.
6   Of the ancient house of Hadloe – whence it passed to the house of Valoigns then, after the reign of King Henry VIII, to Sir Thomas Kempe then to his brother Reginald Kempe, later to Robert Filmer and Sir Dudley Digges (*see further* Chapter 20). In 1689, when Philipott wrote his Villare Cantianum, he records that the mansion was known as Hadloe Place.
7   From 1270 to 1370. Waretius Valoignes then left it to one of his daughters who married Thomas de Aldon whence it passed to the Austen/Austyn family and then in 1590 to Thomas Brodnax – Hasted.

and then, in the early 18th century, to Thomas Brodnax of Hythe (who was also related to the Austen family).[8] It appears therefore that the family of Austen lived in Godmersham some centuries before Thomas Austen, and his more famous sister Jane, ever came there.[9]

It seems strange that the two families, Valoignes and Valence, should have estates so close to each other, and names which, when pronounced, sound almost exactly the same. At a time when names were often spelt a variety of different ways, one might think this more than coincidence. I have not, however, found any blood ties between the two families so this must remain a passing curiosity.

It is striking how the same names and places keep cropping up in the tale of Eggarton; Brabourne is a recurrent visitor.[10] Patterns of family and place names emerge and, like the uncovering of an 'old master', you scrape away and scrape away at the surface until a picture gradually emerges. A chapter is devoted to it here, however, since its story throws light onto Eggarton, and lends credence to the theory that Eggarton was indeed first owned by Aymer's father William.

Lytton Strachey, that master of history, once described historical research as casting a net down into the depths of the profound ocean, fishing up a minnow wriggling and squirming to the light of day and, from this tiny thing, recreating an entire world. Today as we trawl the internet we can fish further and deeper than ever before, yet still the little facts which are caught are entirely arbitrary, and to make so much from so little is entirely presumptuous. Yet presume we must, so here is the story of Brabourne, as derived from the few facts fished out of the ocean of history.

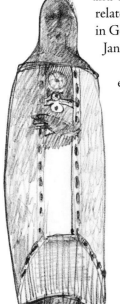

41   *The black Madonna.*

Brabourne is another ancient manor, six miles south-east of Eggarton, and one whose history is intimately connected with it. Perhaps then we should not be surprised to see that it is joined to Eggarton by the ancient North Downs ridgeway.[11]

In the 13th century William de Valence died at his Manor in Brabourne.[12] Half a millennium later, we find that a number of Jane Austen's letters are edited by a relative: the First Baron Brabourne. What is the connection? By dint of much scraping away at family trees we can finally establish a family link, across 500 years, between William de Valence, our great man of action, and Jane Austen our great woman of letters.[13] Today more people are familiar with Jane than with William, which just goes to prove: 'the pen is mightier than the sword'.

Brabourne (named after its broad bourne or stream)[14] was originally part of the lands of the monastery of St Augustine. Following the Norman Conquest it was given to Hugo

8   In the aisle of Crundale church is a tomb stone for 'Anne Broadnax, daughter of William Broadnax, died 1794'.
9   In early times members of the Valoignes family took the name de Ford after the Manor of Ford.
10   It is said that an Anglo-Saxon toponymic will usually lead to a village, while a Norman one will lead to a lordship or castle.
11   Brabourne is a very ancient seat, dating back to a lady called Salburga who died in 864. Later, in the reign of King Henry I it was owned by Robert de Montfort.
12   The Kent Hundred Rolls state that King John held Braybourne Manor through escheat and now the Lord William de Valence holds that manor and has pleas of distraint upon goods and the gallows and the assize of bread and ale.
13   *See* Chapter 18.
14   From Bradebourne – the broad bourne.

de Montfort, together with 30 other nearby manors and estates.[15] Although Eggarton is not named in Domesday Book it is quite possible that it too (a mere six miles distant) was part of the estates granted to Hugo de Montfort, since the whole of Kent was parcelled out among just 13 Norman lords. William de Valence, who later acquired Brabourne, was one of the arch-enemies of the de Montfort family. Ownership of the respective De Montfort and Valence estates in Kent passed regularly back and forth, keeping pace with the fortunes of the war between the King, supported by the Lords of Valence, and the Barons, led by Simon de Montfort. Brabourne and Eggarton were two of the pawns in this national power play.

The manor of Brabourne was passed down from Hugo through further de Montforts, and others, to Simon de Montfort, Earl of Leicester.[16] Simon died leading the Barons at the Battle of Evesham, when they were defeated by William de Valence and the army of King Henry III. His wife, Eleanor, and her children had to flee the realm, lost their estates and died in poverty.[17]

Joane de Munchese married William de Valence; her brother, William de Munchese, chose the wrong side when he fought with the Barons against King Edward I and his own brother-in-law William. The Barons lost, and to punish him, Edward confiscated his estates and gave them to William's sister Joan, and through her to her husband, William de Valence. William de Valence may be excused for feeling he had done rather well out of these arrangements. Not only had he married William de Munchese's sister but he had taken over William's estates – not ideal perhaps for close family relations. Joane, a wealthy heiress, was a good match for William. Having lost his land in France he was looking to pick up estates in England; Joane, a wealthy heiress, was just the person to give them to him. Through her, William became Earl of Pembroke and acquired Brabourne and many other manors besides.[18] Whether or not the estates he gained included Eggarton, I have not been able to discover. The lords of Valence consolidated their land-holdings in Kent, and elsewhere, by virtue of backing the winning team – and this must have gone some way to making up for the loss of their lands in Anjou.

On William de Valence's death in 1296, at Brabourne, the Manor reverted to Joane, and on her death, in 1308, it passed to her son Aymer. On Aymer's death, he left Brabourne to one of his nephews, John Comyn of Badenagh, son of his sister Joane, while his other nephew, John de Hastings, son of his sister Isabel, acquired Eggarton. The Duke of Valence and his family clearly had a real connection with this part of Kent, since his widow, Marie de St Pol, is recorded as living on in Brabourne after the death of her husband.

On the following page is a family tree and time line showing the passage of ownership of Brabourne Manor down from William de Valence through the Strathbogies to the Scotts

---

15   As recorded in Domesday Book.

16   Through Robert de Ver, Henry de Essex, the Priory of Horton, and Baldwin de Betun, Earl of Albemarle. In 1204 Baldwin granted it to William de Mareschal, Earl of Pembroke, on the marriage of Baldwin's daughter Alice to him. In 1226 William, Earl of Pembroke, having buried Alice, re-married Eleanor, King Henry III's sister. William died in 1231 whereupon Eleanor re-married Simon de Montfort, Earl of Leicester.

17   On Simon's death the Brabourne estate would have reverted to William de Marshal, of the Marshal Earls of Pembroke, but since he and his four sons had died, his estate passed to his five daughters, and one of them, Joan, acquired Brabourne. Joan then married Warine de Munchese (or Montchensie) and had a son, William de Munchese, and a daughter Joane de Munchese. Joane married William de Valence.

18   There seems at least a good possibility that Eggarton was part of the original estate of Hugo de Montfort (after all, one of the 13 Kentish lords must have owned it), which then got passed down to the Montchensie family and thence to the Lords of Valence.

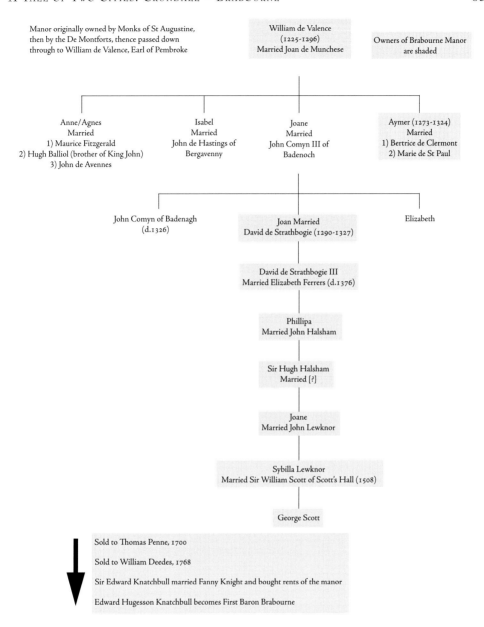

42   *Owners of Brabourne Manor.*

to the Knatchbulls.[19] For those interested in family connections, provides the chain linking together Aymer de Valence, our man of action, with Jane Austen, our woman of letters.

19   John Comyn died in 1326 (murdered by his cousin Robert the Bruce) and left Brabourne manor to his sister Joane, from whom it passed into the ownership of her husband David de Strathbogie. In him, the three great Manors of Eggarton, Brabourne and Chilham, were, for a time, united under the ownership of one man (*see further* Chapter 19). Brabourne passed on through the hands of a number of Strathbogies, through Lord Halsham, Sir William Scott of Scott's Hall (whose family feature prominently in the story of Eggarton under Cromwell and the Stuarts), William Deedes, and finally to Sir Edward Knatchbull who married Fanny Knight, niece of Jane Austen, in 1787. Their son, Edward Hugesson Knatchbull, became First Baron Brabourne and editor of his great aunt Jane's letters – and here, finally, is the link between the Dukes of Valence and Jane Austen.

XIII

HILLES AND VALENCES

At this juncture Eggarton comes into contact with other colourful families perched in different branches of the wider Lusignan family tree.

Aymer's two nephews (both called John) through his sisters Isabel (wife of John de Hastings) and Joane (wife of John Comyn of Badenagh) were his co-heirs. It seems that Isabel's son (John de Hastings) was the one who inherited Eggarton, only to die within a year and leave it to his cousin Joanne, daughter of John Comyn of Badenagh and wife of David de Strathbogie, Earl of Athol and Strathbogie.

The reader, like the writer, may be excused for becoming confused at this juncture. It seems that whenever any of the Lusignans had to name an heir, they confined themselves to names beginning with J. The sons became Johns (after their fathers) while the daughters became Joans (after their mothers). The situation only became resolved when Joan, daughter of Joan (de Valence) daughter of Joan (de Munchese), inherited Eggarton from her cousin John (de Hastings), son of John (de Hastings), son of Joan (de Munchese), in 1325. Joan married someone with a new name – David de Strathbogie – who took over the estate. When they had a son he was not named John but, rather imaginatively, David (de Strathbogie). Accordingly when David de Strathbogie died in the first year of King Edward III's reign (1327) his son, David de Strathbogie, inherited the Eggarton estate.[1] The only real way to make sense of all this is to refer to the Lusignan family tree – which can be found at p.52.[2]

---

[1]   The Monarchy of course have long had this problem: 'The King is dead. Long live the King'. They resolved it by giving themselves numbers as well as names.

[2]   The Earldom of Strathbogie (or Strathbolgie as it is sometimes written) was an ancient one stretching back to a time prior to the Norman Conquest. King Duncan of Scotland first conferred it on his son Malcolm Canmore. Malcolm then came to the Scottish throne in 1058, as King Malcolm III, and married Queen Margaret of Scotland (known as Margaret the Saxon Saint). It was then passed through to Thomas Fitztheobald, Baron de Hilles and Earl of Strathbogie, who married Agnes a Becket, sister of Thomas a Becket, Archbishop of Canterbury, in the 12th century. Thomas it was, who was murdered on the steps within his own cathedral, by three knights who had come from King Henry II.

This litany of Johns, Joans, and Davids does, however, reveal an important difference between the way in which people in medieval times viewed themselves and the way in which modern people view themselves. In medieval times people saw themselves as part of a continuum. Just as they were happy to inherit their estates from their forebears (and pass them on intact to their children) so they were happy to inherit their names. They were part of an ongoing tradition and were proud to be one in a continuing line. Today people are keen to assert their individuality and to strike out and make their own way in the world. Today they want their own names and lives. Today transfers of estates are driven more by the laws of commerce and the market – not testament and family. It was to take a fraud and a bankruptcy (in the reign of King Charles II) to break this family link at Eggarton.

Having inherited Eggarton in the first year of King Edward III's reign (1327), David de Strathbogie, in the seventh year of Edward III's reign (1334), made it over as a gift to 'his kinsman Sir Henry de Hilles'. Eggarton still remained therefore within the extended family and the Kent connection continued. The Hilles is another ancient and important family, connected to Kent and Scotland, and their coat of arms is carved on the walls of Canterbury Cathedral. The Hilles and Strathbogies were related to each other through Thomas Fitztheobold, Baron de Hilles and Earl of Strathbogie and husband of Agnes a Becket.[3]

From Sir Henry de Hilles, Eggarton passed down to many further Hilles – descendants of Sir Henry himself and his brother Gilbert de Hilles who was buried in Godmersham church, beneath a tombstone (now lost) enscribed with his figure in a coat of armour. Gilbert endowed and built a chantry chapel in the southern apse of Godmersham church in 1363 where, for an annual payment of 26s. 8d., a chaplain would 'pray for their [sic family's] good estate whilst still alive and for their souls after death'.[4]

This type of arrangement, or intercession, was very useful to the medieval church. The church had somehow managed to sell the idea that, provided you had adequate funds, you could buy your way into the Kingdom of Heaven. Since direct payment was not possible the church helpfully agreed to accept payment personally and to intercede with the almighty on behalf of the benefactor. This arrangement, as can be imagined, was very convenient to the average knight at the time, allowing them to go about their business fighting wars and oppressing serfs without distraction.

Eggarton, with the intervention of these chantry prayers, enjoyed a peaceable period of 250 years under the stewardship of the Hilles. The Hilles family remained a family of significance throughout, sending representatives to Parliament in Westminster. Eggarton thus stayed in the family until the time of Queen Elizabeth I when, in 1574, Charles Scott, the eldest son of Sir Reginald, or Reynold, Scott of Scotts Hall in Kent, and grandson of Sir Bryan Tuke, Secretary to Cardinal Wolsey, bought the estate for £1,000.[5]

Around the turn of the century, both the great houses of the parish, Eggarton and Forde (or Godmersham), were rebuilt by their owners, reflecting the growing affluence of the times – and, perhaps, a little local rivalry.[6] The chantry chapel continued to serve as a chapel for Eggarton, and is, no doubt, where the bones of lords of the manor were laid to rest beneath

---

3   The Baron also traced his lineage back to Queen Margaret the Saxon saint, who married King Malcolm III of Scotland – thus were the three families, of Lusignan, Strathbogie and Hille kin (*see* the Valence family tree at p.52).

4   *See* Arthur Hussey, *Kent Chantries* (Kent Records XII, 1932-6),131.

5   *See* notes by S.G. Brade-Birks in the *Church Magazine of Crundale and Godmersham* (October 1961) (Reference Library,Canterbury).

6   Page 16, *The Parish Church of St Laurence, Godmersham: A History*, T. Tatton-Brown.

their tombstones. In the early 17th century Robert Juce, who is recorded as living with Thomas Scott at Eggarton, repaired the chantry chapel 'with tyle and glass' before being laid to rest in it himself. This intercession however failed to deliver lasting (or even eternal) benefits since the chapel fell into disrepair and was later taken down when the church was restored.

The Scott family claimed descent from John Balliol, Regent of Scotland (for whom Balliol College in Oxford is named), and father of John Balliol, 1250-1313, King of Scotland. The Scott family derived their name from this Scottish connection.[7] It can thus be seen that the Scotts were related to the Strathbogies, who were in turn kinsmen of the Hilles who were related to the Dukes of Valence (*see* p.52 – Valence family tree). Once again, therefore, Eggarton stayed in the family.

It is striking how easy it is to draw connections between the early owners of the Eggarton Estate. The manor stayed within the same broad family for three centuries, starting with the Dukes of Valence, through the Strathbogies and Hilles, to the Scotts. Looking at Eggarton we can see, in microcosm, how small the landowning class in England and Scotland must have been in medieval times (Domesday Book shows that in the 11th century all of Kent was divided among only 13 families) and how they were nearly all related one to another. The population of England as a whole (before the Black Death) was only four million. Estates in those days were a matter of family and inheritance, with country seats being handed down for generations.

Remarkably, Eggarton's owners can claim descent from the Kings and Queens of both England (through Queen Isabel d' Angouleme and the Earls of Valence by their kinship with King Henry III and Edward I) and Scotland (both through the Hilles, and their descent from Queen Margaret of Scotland, and also through the Scotts and their descent from King John Balliol of Scotland). Very even-handedly, these families supported our two oldest Universities by founding, respectively, Pembroke College in Cambridge and Balliol College in Oxford (*see* images on p.66 and below). Eggarton can thus boast a proud heritage, having been owned by some of the foremost families in the land, families who influenced the course of history in France, England, Scotland and Wales, and whose tombs and coats of arms adorn the Abbey at Westminster and the Cathedral at Canterbury.

There is a recurrent theme connecting the story of the   Manor at Eggarton in Kent with the history of Scotland. The Earls of Pembroke, the Earls of Athol, the Earls of Strathbogie, the Baron Hilles, and the Scotts of Scott Hall, whose families owned Eggarton, all feature in the Scottish annals, and this Scottish link, in a small way, is continued today. My own family hails from Scotland.[8]

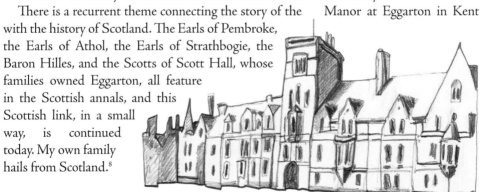

43   *Balliol College.*

7   They were in fact Balliols in disguise. *See further* Chapter 19.
8   My family's connection with Queen Margaret the Saxon saint was, however, less happy. She reputedly gave away half of the ancient Lands of Ballingall to the monks of the island of May off the Firth of Forth in the 11th century. This will have been in some ancient form of conveyance, subsequently confirmed by charter by her youngest son King David I.

XIV

THE RESTORATION (AND LOSS)

Dorothea Scott and the Bankruptcy of Eggarton

After two and a half relatively uneventful centuries Charles Scott bought Eggarton from the Hilles family and, in 1635, the Manor passed down to Dorothea Scott, his grand-daughter. As England descended into the chaos of civil war, Eggarton once again became caught up in events which swept the country. It is a tale which could not be stranger had it been invented.

It involves a Roundhead major, a restored monarch, the Duke of York, an unholy villain, a famous diarist, the Tower of London, fraud, lies, abandonment, bankruptcy, bigamy, enslavement, false imprisonment, murder and, finally, new life. History has, once, famously been defined as: 'An account, mostly false, of events, mostly unimportant, which are brought about by rulers, mostly knaves, and soldiers, mostly fools.'[1] This story has all the necessary ingredients of history and deserves a book to be written about it.[2] It has, at any rate, its own chapter, which follows.

Dorothea Scott was born in the year 1611,[3] baptised in Godmersham church on 22 September, and died 77 years later, on 10 April 1688, on the other side of the world, in Oyster Bay, Nassau, New York. When her father, Thomas Scott,[4] died in 1635, closely followed by her mother and brother (also Thomas), Dorothea unexpectedly inherited the estate of Eggarton. She also gained an early acquaintance with the court when, at the age of 24, still grieving for her parents and brother, she had to fight off a claim to

---

1   Ambrose Bierce.
2   Indeed a private publication was made of the life of Dorothea Scott in a pamphlet entitled ' Dorothea Scott, otherwise Gotherson and Hogben, of Egerton House Kent: 1611-1680' by G.D. Scull, printed by Parker and Co., Oxford, 1883 (and kept, formerly, in the library of The Society of Friends (Quakers), Devonshire House, London).
3   Confusingly, 'A Noble Birthright,' at userpages.burgoyne.com, gives a different birth date of 1628/9. It would appear that the author confused Dorothea with another relative of the same name.
4   Charles Scott, 1543-96 (son of Sir Reginald Scott 1511-44, of Scotts Hall, head of the family), bought Eggarton and left it to his son Thomas Scott 1567-1635, who married Mary Jane Knatchbull. He left it to his eldest son Thomas Scott, 1605-35, who quickly died and left it to his sister Dorothea (*see* Scott family tree, p.72). The Scotts were a royal and ancient family claiming descent from John Balliol regent of Scotland (for whom Balliol College Oxford is named), father of John Balliol (1250-1313) King of Scotland.

44   *Land use in a typical medieval manor.*

the estate brought by other relatives. This stood her in good stead for other legal battles she would have to fight during her long and eventful life. The Eggarton estate at this time, as described in the will of Thomas Scott,[5] comprised: 'The Manor of Eggarton with 4 messuages, 2 granaries, 1 dovecote, 3 orchards, and 336 acres of land in Godmesham, Crundale, Wye and Waltham, held of the Dean and Chapter of Canterbury under the Manor of Godmesham, Value 8 li, and 66 other acres under the manor of Godmersham, value 20 shillings.'[6]

The estate which she inherited carried with it the goodly income of £500 per annum; Dorothea was, in short, worth marrying. So, at any rate, thought Daniel Gotherson (also known as Gutherson), a major in Cromwell's army, who snapped her up shortly following her brother's death. This was very convenient for him since in the following year, 1636, his merchant's business in Southwark descended into bankruptcy.

5   As held in the Kent County Archives at Maidstone, Kent. The archives also hold a fine deed of Michaelmas 1654 (19 years later) describing the estate as 'The manor at Eggarton with 4 messuages, 2 cottages, 4 barns, 1 dovehouse, 4 gardens, 4 orchards, 260 acres of land, 40 pastures, 20 meadows and 40 wood.' A messuage was a dwelling house together with its outbuildings and land.
6   As part of his will in 1635 Thomas Scott also endowed a Poor House in Godmersham village.

Set out opposite is a picture of how a typical manor estate would be farmed in Dorothea's times, and we can take it that the Manor of Eggarton followed this pattern.[7]

Life continued and the Gothersons started a family. They were well connected and, one fateful day in 1661, went to pay court to the recently restored monarch, Charles II. Here, in Whitehall, they met one John Scott in the company of the King. To this ill-starred meeting can be traced the downfall of the family. As well as sharing a family name with them, John Scott's features (as Dorothea later recalled in testimony) bore a certain resemblance to the Scott physiognomy. Relying on this, John Scott ingratiated himself with the family, posing as a relative and even, for a time, living under the same roof as them. The story he spun was that he had been deported to America as a boy 'for cutting ye soldier's girths of their saddles that were against ye King and such like'. Here he managed to free himself and took up with the natives in Long Island, making his fortune and buying great tracts of land there. Impressed by this tale, Major Gotherson paid John Scott a considerable sum of money to purchase 20,000 acres of land on Long Island and to build two homes on it, intending that the family should start a new life out there. He also entrusted his only son, Daniel, to his keeping. Scott was to take him to America, ensure his education, and set him up in the houses to await the arrival of the rest of the family. Perhaps, once Cromwell died and King Charles II had been restored to the throne, life in England for a former Major in Cromwell's New Model Army, and a Quaker to boot, was too difficult. A new life in the New World beckoned. Unfortunately on 1 September 1666, just prior to the Great Fire of London, Daniel Gotherson died. Dorothea was left a widow with five daughters to look after and an inheritance of heartache and woe from her husband.

Daniel Gotherson, in throwing in his lot with Cromwell and his New Model Army had, ultimately, backed the wrong side (though he later tried to make amends by turning informant on his erstwhile colleagues).[8] He was not a man of judgement. After the war he bankrupted his business and later, at his untimely death, ruined his family.

Looking into his affairs, Dorothea was appalled to find that the Eggarton estate had been mortgaged to creditors for £6,000.[9] Her investigations seemed to show that Major Gotherson had paid John Scott £2,000 for 20,000 acres of land in New York which he claimed to have bought from the Indian Chiefs there. Scott had taken their money and their son, but some question now arose about their title to the land on Long Island. John Scott, needless to say, at this stage, was nowhere to be found. Dorothea feared the worst – no land, no money, no son, no husband, no inheritance, no John Scott. Many questions: no answers.

It was left for Dorothea to pick up the pieces and try to put them together again. This was no mean task. Today it is easy to find things out with the benefit of the internet, the telephone, a postal service, an aeroplane service and a police service to help us – all the advantages, in fact, of modern life. In the 17th century, Dorothea enjoyed none of these. America was three months away by boat. Dorothea had a family of five girls in England to support, not to mention a son in America to find. She had lost her husband, her son and,

---

7   Taken from a *Historical Atlas* by William R. Shepherd, 1929 edition.

8   It seems latterly that he passed on information to the King about possible anti-monarchist plotters in Kent.

9   The Kent County Archives in Maidstone hold a number of mortgages including one of 14 October 1663 for £5,000.

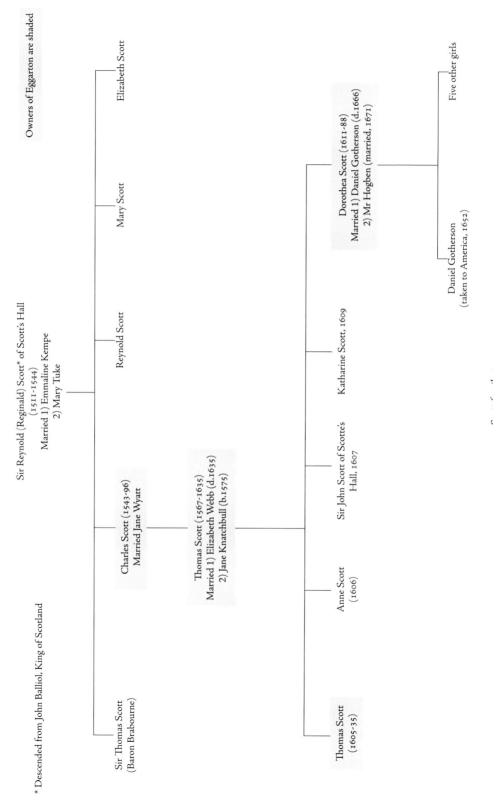

* Descended from John Balliol, King of Scotland

Owners of Eggarton are shaded

Sir Reynold (Reginald) Scott* of Scott's Hall
(1511-1544)
Married 1) Emmaline Kempe
2) Mary Tuke

Sir Thomas Scott
(Baron Brabourne)

Charles Scott (1543-96)
Married Jane Wyatt

Reynold Scott

Mary Scott

Elizabeth Scott

Thomas Scott (1567-1635)
Married 1) Elizabeth Webb (d.1635)
2) Jane Knatchbull (b.1575)

Thomas Scott
(1605-35)

Anne Scott
(1606)

Sir John Scott of Scotte's
Hall, 1607

Katharine Scott, 1609

Dorothea Scott (1611-88)
Married 1) Daniel Gotherson (d.1666)
2) Mr Hogben (married, 1671)

Daniel Gotherson
(taken to America, 1652)

Five other girls

45   *Scott family tree.*

in all likelihood, her house and property; creditors were at the door and the villain who had ruined her had disappeared. She was, however, made of sterner stuff than her husband. She kept her creditors at bay with the income from her mortgaged estate (all of which, she complained, went to service the debt), while she tried to establish what had happened.

Today, nearly 400 years later, thanks to the records kept by the courts and by Samuel Pepys (the great chronicler of his time) we can piece together a picture of events more easily than she could – and this is what we find.

John Scott was a chancer. He had no blood connection with the Scotts of Scott Hall at all, but had used the coincidence of sharing a name to pass himself off as a lost relative returning as a wealthy man from the Americas. In fact he was flat broke and fleeing the law. He insinuated himself into the family with an eye to relieving them of their fortune, and poor Major Gotherson (having lost one fortune and married another) was just the man to give it to him.

It transpired that, in addition to being wanted by Dorothea for cheating her of her inheritance in England, he was separately wanted for frauds in New England, Barbados, France, and Holland. He was a consummate international fraudster and, like so many confidence tricksters, when you wanted him, he was nowhere to be found. When things got difficult in one country, John Scott simply moved to another.

Nearly everyone that came across John Scott had cause to regret it. He was a man who contributed considerably to the sum of human misery. His story is strewn with corpses, abandoned wives, ruined families, betrayed countries. Often, if you look hard enough, it is possible to find some redeeming feature in the most desperate of villains: some are kind to their mothers, others love animals, others again are loyal to their partners in crime. None of these saving graces can be found in the villain Scott.

He was, however, a man of ability. He started life, with few advantages, in Ashford 'of meane parents' – the son of an impoverished miller. He was shipped to New England as a boy to make his way in the New World and he used his wits to drag himself up.

'Hee having a nimble genius, though otherwise illiterate, with the helpe of a little reading and having a good memory to retaine the same and great confidence, hee became somewhat above the common people.'[10]

An unusual amount can be discovered about him as a result of his dealings with Samuel Pepys. From the meticulous notes kept by that great chronicler of his times, a record of the man and his career can be pieced together. It appears (slightly updated) overleaf.

Though utterly ruthless, he must have had charm. His rise owed much to his ability to make friends, and gain patrons, in high places. Having initially bettered himself in the New World 'upon newes of the King's restoration in England, hee found means to be transported over to England.' Here he reinvented himself, and gained the friendship of Thomas Chiffinch, page of the closet of King Charles II and 'Keeper of his Rarities'. Through Thomas he made the acquaintance of Sir Joseph Williamson (Secretary to Lord Arlington the Secretary of State). This friend at Court gave him the entrée to society that he needed. While at Court one fateful day he made the acquaintance of Dorothea Gotherson and her husband Daniel, who had come to pay their respects to the new King – from that moment their fate was sealed.

---

10   Testimony of Captain Mathias Nicholls. *See* G.D. Scull's publication, footnote 2 above.

'Curriculum Vitae' of the villain John Scott

1632   Born in Ashford 'of very mean parentage'

1643   Emigrates to New England, America; educated at the School of Hard Knocks

1650   Higher Education: School for Villains
        Chosen specialisation: fraud
        Work experience:
                – Long Island (property fraud)
                – Rhode Island (property fraud)
                – Atherton Land Company (embezzlement)
        Special interests/hobbies: impersonation, fraud, slander, laying false witness, ruination, bigamy, child trafficking, murder and spying

1660   Further education (overseas in England):
        Impersonation (as long lost Scott relative)
                – Sponging (living in the Scott household)
                – Child Abduction (of Daniel Gotherson junior)
                – Deception (cheating Gothersons out of £6,000)
        Domestic project: abandoning mother to life of destitution

1663   Graduates 'cum laude'. Returns to New England

1664   Pursues career as fraudster, defrauding the Gothersons of 20,000 acres in Long Island
        Flees to Barbados
                – Abandons first wife with no means of support
                – sells Daniel Gotherson (Junior) into servitude

1664/5 Serves as Captain in Sir Tobias Smith's regiment in Barbados

1668   Appointed Geographer to King Charles II
        Takes a second wife in England (bigamously)
        Abandons second wife. Flees to Holland

1668   Continues career as fraudster in the Netherlands
        Embarks on second career as international spy

1672   Flees the Netherlands
        Convicted in absence of £7,000 fraud
        Burnt in effigy in Le Hague

1673   Enters service of the Prince of Conde (France) as a spy

1678   Arrested in England as a spy
        Lays false evidence against Samuel Pepys
        Pepys is committed to The Tower
        Murders a London magistrate
        Escapes

1682   Returns to London disguised as a Jesuit priest
        Murders George Butler (a hackney coachman)
        Escapes to Norway

1696   Pardoned by King William and returns to England

[?]   Dies in his bed – a free man

Epitaph A fondly remembered graduate of the School for Villains, John Scott did much to raise the profile of fraudsters everywhere – putting the art of cheating persons and governments on a truly international basis for the first time. John Scott lost no opportunity, throughout his rich and varied life, of putting into practice these arts he learnt so well at school. In addition to the financial frauds at which he was so adept, John Scott also found time for spying (for a number of different sovereign states – simultaneously), bigamy, child slavery, laying false witness, perjury, impersonation, and murder. He is an example to villains the world over.

46 'Curriculum Vitae' of the villain John Scott.

He wormed his way into the confidence of the Gotherson household. Having gained their trust he persuaded Major Gotherson to pay him £2,000 for 20,000 acres of land on Long Island (owned, as it subsequently transpired, by the local Indians and not by Mr Scott). He took young Daniel Gotherson to Long Island with him, together with materials and carpenters from England – all subsequently paid for by Dorothea in England, following the death of her husband in 1666. When in New York, John Scott took the opportunity to commit further frauds which, when discovered, obliged him to flee the country.

John Scott was forced to depart for England again in such haste that he failed to take his wife (whom he had omitted to mention to anyone) with him, leaving her destitute and in a foreign country. Thus the villain had made two different women (his wife, and Dorothea) destitute on two different continents. To make matters worse for Dorothea, the two houses which had been built on Long Island were then dismantled (since there was no right to build on the land) and given by Mr Nicholls, the then Governor of New York, for rebuilding in Seatalcott, for the relief of John Scott's deserted wife.[11]

In the midst of these shenanigans, young Daniel Gotherson (Dorothea's son) very sensibly escaped from John Scott and hid in a wood. John Scott, not bothering to find him, left instructions with a Mr Herringmen of New Haven (where he was staying) that he could take the boy in if he turned up, and use him as he willed. Following Scott's departure, Daniel came out of hiding and Mr Herringmen promptly indentured him, setting him to work in the yard. Daniel Gotherson was thus, instead of being educated at a school in America, consigned to a life of servitude in a stable yard.[12] John Scott was a man who played havoc with the lives of those who came across him.

John Scott fled post haste to England in 1664 where he coolly reported to Major Gotherson (just before his death) that the boy was safely delivered and the houses duly built. Then, before matters in America and England could catch up with him, he escaped to Holland.

Meanwhile back in Kent, in 1667, with her husband laid to rest in his grave and John Scott vanished, Dorothea was endeavouring to discover the state of affairs in Long Island. Dorothea's hope still was to sell Eggarton and move to New England. Dorothea was a lady of character. Although, of her early youth, she admitted that she did 'eat of the forbidden fruit and transgress God's laws'. This did not prevent her from becoming a Quaker, and, indeed, in due course a minister. She went on to form a congregation called (after her family name) 'Scott's Congregation'. She now planned to emigrate with her family and her Quaker congregation, reunite herself with her son and kiss goodbye to England – leaving her troubles behind her.

New England was, at this time, an English colony. Sir Francis Lovelace had been appointed as the new Governor and in November 1667, as he set out to take up his position, Dorothea approached him to look into the matter of the land in Long Island; she gave him a power of attorney authorising him to investigate matters in her name. In order to encourage him in this task she wrote, according to court records, as follows:

---

11   Other documents suggest that the timber was forfeit to Joseph Rayner and Richard Harding of Boston in satisfaction of considerable debts owed to them. It is not known which is correct.

12   It had been planned that the governor of New York would arrange for young Daniel's education, and to pay for this, Major Gotherson had assigned to the Governor a debt for £500 – owed to him by John Scott. Needless to say, the debt was never paid and the assignment was worth nothing.

The should [sic] inducement to Governor Lovelace to take upon himselfe ye Trouble of Mrs Gotherson's business at New-York, was a promise shee made him at his going, that if shee could make any money by the sale of her Land in Kent, which had been mortgaged by her husband in his lifetime, shee would herselfe go over to New-Yorke and carry an hundred and twenty Familes with her to ye great advantage of ye Place.

Dorothea was very energetic in bending the ear of authority. While it is quite possible that Governor Lovelace viewed the prospect of Dorothea's arrival in New York as a 'great advantage of ye place' it is also possible that he saw it as something of a mixed blessing. The next person who Dorothea attempted to enlist in her cause was the Governor's brother, Thomas Lovelace. The next year, following after his brother, Thomas was going out to reconnoitre New England and planned to return later that year to collect his family and emigrate. Dorothea was desperate for any news from New England, thus Thomas became the recipient of one of Dorothea's forthright letters in March 1668:

47   *Dorothea's petition.*

> My Friend,
> … be pleased to give notice by my Daughter when thou intends to depart from England, that soe I may repair to London again … I have bin at London neer three weeks waiting thy coming, because thou told me thy intentions were to be heer in February. I have sent every week to the Butcher's Arms since to enquire of thy coming, and they have sent me word every weeke, they look for thee, but since I see thee not nescesity calls me home … I have bin put to great straits, and have and doe live in hopes to see all sold here, and then, and not till then, will it be determined what will be afforded me and my six children, but naked we must returne, and still blesse his name whose protection I commit thee unto, and remain thy trewe friend, and could serve thee if it were in my power. I am knowne to thee by the name of Dorothea Gotherson.

Dorothea was a resourceful lady, and was not going to let a small thing like the death of a husband or the loss of an inheritance stand in the way of the plans she had for herself and her congregation. The Scott family still had connections and she decided to 'go to the top' – she petitioned the King. It was a slow business however ascertaining what happened in America and gaining an audience with the King in England. The King's Secretary asked Dorothea to write down the facts of the matter, which she did as follows:

> Lett it please the King to know that I formerly Dorothea Scott being heire to the yoonger house of Scotts Hall in Kent did match with Daniell Gotherson to whom I brought ye estate of neer 500 pounds per annum which estate being all morgaged by my husband and since his death all extended for debt soe that my selfe and six chilldren crave ye kings clemency in the case following …

> A great part of my husbands debts being contracted by his disbursing near two thousand pounds to one John Scott for land and houses in Long Island which land is all disposed of and ye houses pulled downe and sett up in other places and my son for whome ye land was bought exposed to work for bread ye 2 or 3 years last past who is not yett full seventeen years of age.

> Lett it please ye King therfore to give his Royall Letter of order to ye now deputy governour Francis Lovelasse to examine my prefections and doe justlie and if it appear I have noe interest in land ther I have none elswhere yett blessed be his name who oblige me to wish ye Kings eternall wellfare as my owne and many more such unfeigned true subjects as Dorothea Gotherson.

Her own peculiar brand of bludgeon, religion and flattery paid off, and in May she was rewarded with an audience with the King: Charles II. She spent half an hour with him, explaining her plight, after which time the King's brother, the Duke of York, happened to be passing through the adjacent room. Seizing on this opportunity (with some relief I suspect) the King explained that it would not be proper for him (the King) to address the Governor of New York on this matter, and suggested that his brother, the Duke of York, might handle it. To his credit, the Duke of York agreed to look into the matter, and deputed his secretary, Mr Wren, to write a letter to the Governor, which he did as follows:

> Sir, This Gentlewoman Mrs. Dorothy Gotherson having complained to his Royal Highness of some hard usage she hath mett with in some Business of hers at New York, His Royal highness hath thereupon commanded mee to write unto you that you will cause her Pretensions to be examined and doe her Right in her affaires. I am your most humble servant,

Thus Thomas Lovelace set out for America, armed with a deposition from Dorothea in his pocket, together with a letter of instruction from Mr Wren for his brother, Francis, the new Governor of New York. Thomas was at first suspicious that Dorothea (or her husband) may themselves have been involved in some skulduggery. Dorothea had to convince him that she had played no part in any deception (and indeed that she was the victim of the crime). He was, however, persuaded by Dorothea's own inimitable brand of advocacy:

> My esteemed friend, Coll, Lovelace,
>
> … I intreat thee to doe what lieth in thy power for thy country people (viz.) myselfe and Chilldren, and thyselfe shall see if I am of ability that I shall not be ungratefull; and seeing providence hath caste my sonne one thy care, I leave him wholly under God to thy ordering …

> I did not deale underhand for Scott to make him any interest ther … I have not seen John Scott neere six yeare. I entreate thee to read this ould writing, wch is on account of thy horses, and now I am straightened for time.[13] Otherwise I should have new writ that particular – now my friend it is in my hert to stir up thy mind to doe good to all in thy place, as thou art a Minister of Justice, and to love and delight in mercy, for I am certain the time is begun againe that bloodthirsty men and persecutors shall not live out half their daies. Dear friend, I speak by way of caution, not of accusation, for I hope thou art otherwise inclined, but fearing least at any time thou might be stirred up by ye enemy of ye soule[14] to doe his work; this is what I have to writ, and I hope it will be reseaved in love and good will, as it is written by her who is known to thee by the name of,

> Dorothea Gotherson ye 15 of the moneth called June – London.

---

13   This is a peculiarly original excuse for poor writing, on a par perhaps with the modern school boy equivalent: 'I am sorry sir, the dog ate my homework'.

14   The Devil.

In the face of such arguments, the Governor was persuaded. He wrote advising Dorothea to come to America herself to look into the matter. Dorothea refused, saying that she had five children to look after and anyway had no money. Finally, however, the Governor was persuaded into action and managed to lay bare John Scott's fraudulent activity. On investigating the land in Long Island the Governor found that John Scott had never owned it, and therefore could not sell it; sadly nothing could be done about this.

In a deposition the Governor wrote:

> Mrs Dorothea Scott, heiresse to £500 per annum, of Scott's–hall, in ye County of Kent, and relict of Major Daniel Gotherson the Ellder of Egerton in the said county, havinge received many pretended kindnesses from one Titular Major John Scott of Long Island in America, did entrust him with the whole concernes of her estate, which in the end proved fatall to her, … upon strict inquiry made, the said Commissioners found the ould proverb verified, 'Where nothing is to be had, the King must lose his right'.

Dorothea was faced with the worst of all worlds: no money (John Scott had pocketed that) and no promised land in America. Colonel Thomas Lovelace did, however, discover young Daniel in servitude at *Herringman's Inn* in New Haven, rubbing down horses in the yard. He must by this time have been won over by Dorothea's own peculiar brand of rhetoric and out of the goodness of his heart he paid £7 to free the boy, bought him some clothes, and sent him to school in New York. For a while it seemed that Daniel's fortunes had taken a turn for the better, but the providence which Dorothea was such a strong believer in was not so kind to her son. After his schooling he sought to return to England to see his mother and family. Sadly Dorothea was never to see him again. In a court document she later laments, 'but now it is thought and I have long feared [he] is cast away with Joseph Freeman's ship coming from ye Barbadoes'.

It is interesting to consider what might have been had John Scott been acting in good faith and the Gothersons achieved their plan to exchange their own estate in Godmersham for 20,000 acres of real estate in New York. Major Gotherson would have got the better part of the deal, acquiring what was to become the most valuable land in the world, worth, today, many billions of dollars, in return for some relatively poor farming land in East Kent. Sadly, this was not the future that Dorothea was facing in 1669.

The Duke of York had become interested in the affair and, in particular, with the nefarious and elusive Mr John Scott. He took it on himself to command Samuel Pepys, then Secretary to the Admiralty, to collect evidence against Scott. Mr Pepys it was, who uncovered a chain of deceit stretching from New England, to Barbados, France, Holland and England. John Scott was a fraudster on a truly international scale. Indeed such was his reputation in Le Hague, where he had defrauded the Dutch Government of £7,000, that in 1672 he was convicted in absence and burnt in effigy.

Finding things a little too hot in the Netherlands, John Scott returned to London in disguise as a Jesuit priest where, in 1678, he proceeded to murder a London magistrate. Samuel Pepys now had assembled enough evidence against him and moved to commit John Scott. The following description of the man was given out:

> He has one or both legs crooked, a proper well-sett man, in a great light cockered Perriwig, rough visaged, having large haire on his eyebrows, hollow eyed, a little squinting or a cast with his eye, full faced about ye cheeks, about 46 years of age, with a Black hatt and in a straight boddy'd coat, cloath colour with siver lace behind.

Aided by this colourful description he was apprehended at Folkestone. John Scott, however, was no mean antagonist. On examination he claimed 'that he was a pensioner to the Prince of Condé, and had formerly commanded the said Prince of Condé's regiment of Horse in the French service, and that the said Prince had sent for him in September last in order to oversee the surveying of some lands and woods in Burgundy and Picardy.' Whatever the truth of this, he had friends of influence in England including two persistent enemies of Samuel Pepys: William Harbord and Lord Salisbury. Things came to a head when Samuel Pepys moved to have him arraigned on the charge of murder. John Scott in turn laid evidence against Samuel Pepys that he had betrayed naval secrets to the French and was planning to dethrone the King and to ban the Protestant religion. Lord Shaftesbury used these calumnies to have Pepys committed to the Tower of London on a charge of treason. From there, Pepys had to rely on the good offices of his brother-in-law, Balthazar St Michael, to obtain further evidence in France of John Scott's roguery. Ultimately it was the death-bed admission of Pepys' butler, John James, who, unwilling to meet his maker with calumny on his conscience, confessed that John Scott had induced him to commit perjury against him. Thus Pepys was finally able to discredit John Scott's evidence and clear himself of the trumped-up charge of treason on 12 February 1679.[15]

Events then moved towards their conclusion. Although John Scott was discredited and his villainy laid bare, Dorothea was not able to regain the 20,000 acres of land in Long Island. It transpired, however, that Daniel Gotherson had succeeded in buying 10 acres of land in Oyster Bay from a merchant called John Richbell in 1663, two years before his death, and Dorothea thus inherited this.

Meanwhile, John Scott, undeterred by any of these proceedings, and protected by influential benefactors, went about London disguised as a Jesuit priest, and proceeded to murder a hackney coachman, George Butler, in 1682. In Thompson's Intelligencer of 20 May 1682 the following description accompanied his warrant for apprehension:

> He is a lusty tall man, squint eyed, thin faced, weares a Peruke sometimes, and has a very h … look'.
> Once again, however before being brought to trial (and aided no doubt by friends at court who had
> found Scott useful in all the plots and counter plots that were rife at the time) he managed to escape;
> running out of more convenient countries to flee to, he made his way to Norway.

Scott, whilst 'in his cups' in Skeen, Norway, in 1683 confessed to John Gelson, the skipper of a Norwegian vessel, that he had been a 'toole much used' in the 'villaneous practices that has of late years been in our Nation' and that 'their design was to destroy the Government'. He had been caught up with the odious Titus Oates (who also laid false claims against Pepys) and others of that cabal. Lord Shaftesbury, foremost amongst the plotters, had promised him great settlements.

Perhaps things ended happily for Dorothea after all. She had, by this time, acquired a second husband, Mr Hogben (whom she married in Godmersham church in the year 1671) and was at last able to realise her dream of starting a new life in America. In 1676 Dorothea sold her estate in England in order to pay off her creditors, and Eggarton passed into the hands of the interestingly named Sir James Rushout.[16] With the money raised

---

15   It is not clear if this was in 1679 or 1680.
16   The Kent County Archives in Maidstone hold (a) a final release of claim to a mortgage of 1 June 1676 by George and Dorothy Hogben and Daniel Gotherson the younger (b) a conveyance of 1676 from the same to Sir William Adams and William Jarrett and an immediate on-sale to Sir James Rushout.

Dorothea Scott Timeline

1611	Dorothea Scott born (daughter to Thomas Scott)
1635	Father, mother and brother die. Dorothea inherits Eggarton. Dorothea marries Daniel Gotherson
1661	Dorothea and Daniel first meet the rogue John Scott, at Westminster. He moves in with them
1663	John Scott takes their young son, Daniel, and £2,000 to Long Island, New York, to buy 20,000 acres and build two houses
1664	John Scott returns and reports houses built and boy delivered. In fact, boy was sold into drudgery, £2,000 was stolen, and Scott fled America leaving a wife and scandal behind him
1665	Daniel Gotherson (husband) dies. John Scott flees to Holland. Dorothea left with five daughters, one lost son, and bankrupt estate
1667	Dorothea gives power of attorney to Francis Lovelace, new governor of New York to investigate the property
1668	Thomas Lovelace (Govenor's brother) goes to New York, rescues her son; puts him in school
1669	Dorothea petitions King Charles II. Duke of York looks into it. Fraud laid bare. The Duke later gets S. Pepys to investigate Scot
1671	Dorothea marries Mr Hogben in Godmersham church
1672	John Scott defrauds Dutch government of £7,000, disappears and is hanged in effigy at Le Hague
1678	John Scott, disguised as a Jesuit priest, murders a magistrate in London
1679	John Scott lays false information against Pepys who is confined to the tower.
1680	S. Pepys is released from Tower. Dorothea discovers that Daniel Gotherson did own some acres in Oyster Bay. She sells Eggarton estate, and emigrates to start new life with her family
1682	John Scott kills a hackney carriage driver and flees to Norway
1688	Dorothea dies peacefully in Oyster Bay, Nassau
1696	John Scott is pardoned by King William III and returns to London

from the sale of Eggarton, she paid off her husband's creditors, and had just enough money to emigrate to America with her family, and other Quakers, in 1676. She died 12 years later, after a long and eventful life, on 10 April 1688 in Oyster Bay, Nassau, New York. Set out at the end of this chapter is a timeline, in her memory, showing the principal events of Dorothea Gotherson's life.

John Scott meanwhile continued to enjoy a charmed existence. Incredibly, his friends managed to persuade the new King, William III, to pardon him (along with Titus Oates) and, in 1696, having outlasted Dorothea, he returned to England a free man and without a stain on his character.[17]

Although John Scott did not bring down the indomitable Dorothea, he dealt a blow to the Manor of Eggarton from which it never truly recovered. From here the manor descended into further bankruptcy and, ultimately, destruction. But that is another tale — to which we now turn.

---

17   Life is not always fair. Hopefully, however, the above account will go some way to setting the historical record straight.

XV

THOSE WHO RUSH IN ALSO RUSH OUT
How the Gotts got Eggarton

Sir James Rushout,[1] who bought Eggarton from Dorothea in 1680, acting true to his name, found that his actions had been precipitate. It seems likely that he took down and rebuilt the mansion, over-extending himself in the process.[2] In a letter to his friend Robert Clayton,[3] he complains of the cost of running his estate at Eggarton. His concerns must have been well founded since, when he died, his trustees had to sell the estate for the payment of his debts (just, in fact, as Dorothea had to do after the death of her husband). In any event Mr Peter Gott of Sussex bought the estate from his executors in 1705. Peter passed it on to his descendant, Maximilian, who in turn left it to his three sisters, Sarah, Elizabeth and Mary. In 1758 they were involved in litigation with the Filmers over a lease of the property.[4] This having been resolved, Sarah then lived at Eggarton (following the death of her two sisters) for many years.[5]

When Sarah Gott died, in 1772, she passed on her share of Eggarton Manor in her will to the two daughters of William Western Hugesson of Provender: Mary and Dorothea. They married, respectively, Sir Edward Knatchbull[6] and Sir Joseph Banks. A settlement deed of 1780, entered into after the marriage of Joseph Banks and Dorothea Hugesson, refers to '… the Mansion House called Eggarton, Little Eggarton Farm and other lands and woods in Godmersham and Crundale'. These heiresses, together with the other co-owner, Henry Thomas Gott, sold the Eggarton estate to Thomas Knight of Godmersham.

---

1   Born 1644, died 1699. MP for Evesham and Worcestershire.
2   *See* preface to *Dorothea Scott, otherwise Gotherson and Hogben, of Egerton House Kent: 1611-1680*, by G.D. Scull, printed by Parker and Co., Oxford, 1883.
3   According to the Canterbury archives the letter is dated 1671 – though the date must be too early, since other sources suggest he did not buy the estate until 1680.
4   Filmer v Gott 1758.
5   Letter no.24 of *Letters of Jane Austen, 1800-1801*, Brabourne edition, edited by First Baron Brabourne. *See also* Chapter 8: 'God's Land Surrounded by Water.'
6   The Knatchbulls were subsequently connected with Lord Louis Mountbatten whose nephew is the Duke of Edinburgh, consort to Queen Elizabeth II.

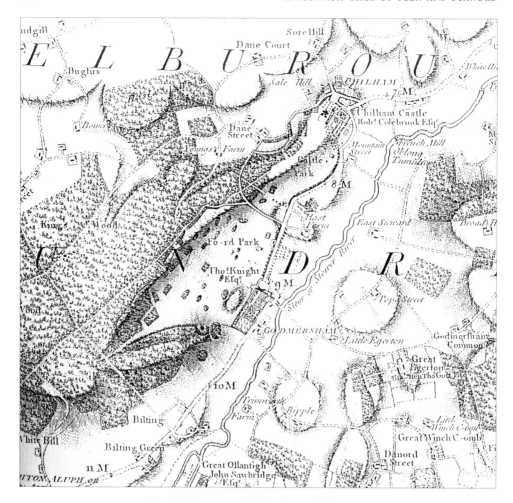

48   *Map showing estates of Godmersham and Eggarton, 1779.*

He bought it in 1780 as a residence for his sister Jane Knight.[7] Jane Knight and her sister Elizabeth were living in Bilting at the time. Ultimately it was Elizabeth who moved (or, perhaps, was moved) into the manor.

The arrangement was described by Thomas Knight's great-grandson, Edward Hugesson Knatchbull, 1st Baron Brabourne, as follows:[8] 'Mrs Elizabeth Knight was of weak intellect, and after the two sisters had resided first at Bilting, she was moved to Eggarton, a larger and more convenient house, and two lady attendants, Miss Cuthbert and her sister Maria, were engaged to look after her.'

Thus began a fateful chapter in the life of the manor as it passed into the hands of the Knight/Austen family of Godmersham Park – to whom we now turn.

---

7   According to *A new and complete History of the county of Kent.* According to Baron Brabourne, however (*see* footnote 8 below), the estate was bought by Jane herself and not by Thomas.

8   *See* Letters of Jane Austen – Brabourne edition. Commentary by First Baron Brabourne.

XVI
KNIGHTS AND AUSTENS

In the 1720s Eggarton's chantry chapel was taken down and Godmersham church was rebuilt. We can see, perhaps, signs of a little local rivalry between the estates of Eggarton and Godmersham with the building of large family pews for each of them, raised above the level of the nave in two grand bays off the southern aisle.[1] Thus the houses of Godmersham and Eggarton from their lofty elevation could look down on the rest of the congregation (*see further* Chapter 8). Some time later the Godmersham estate got the upper hand by installing a personal fire place and chimney in their bay. Though they could not guess it at the time, Eggarton's star was on the wane; Godmersham's was in the ascendant.

At around this time, 1727, Thomas Brodnax (sometimes also spelt Brodnax),[2] who was the owner of the Manor of Ford, changed his name to Thomas May and (with the benefit of a large inheritance from Sir Thomas May) drew up grand plans for the estate. In 1732 he rebuilt the Manor on the site of the earlier Elizabethan house which his family had lived in for some 250 years. He then (with the benefit of a second large inheritance) turned the surrounding 600 acres into parkland, and called it Ford Park.[3] He it was, therefore, who changed the character of the estate from medieval agrarian to country park (a trend which his descendents then pursued – by pulling down the medieval village).

---

1   *See* a note of Monumental Inscriptions in Godmersham church 1757 by Rev. Bryan Fausset, '… on ye South Side of the aisle … are now 2 very large and Handsome Pews for Mr KNIGHTS and Mrs GOTT's familys. Under that of Mr Knight is a very Large Vault for ye Burial of his Family.'

2   The Manor of Ford had been in the ownership of the Brodnax (sometimes spelt Broadnax) family since 1590. There is an iron plate on the south side of the chancel (moved there in the Victorian restoration), on which is recorded: 'Hic jacet Thomas Brodnax qui obijt 5 die Sepembris 1602.'

3   Forde is its ancient name. Beneath the church are ancient vaults for the houses of Ford and Godmersham. The earliest recorded owner was Robert de la Forde (taking his name from the place) who made a grant of land to the Prior and Convent of Christ Church in 1255 (Canterbury Cathedral Archive).

He seems to have been a man unable to settle on a name and keep to it for, in 1738, he changed his name again to Thomas Knight.[4] It seems that it was necessary to go to Parliament to effect his changes of name, and on the second such occasion one of the Members was heard to observe, 'I think we ought to pass an Act of Parliament to allow this gentlemen to call himself anything he pleases'. Thomas married Jane Monk and had a son, also called Thomas Knight, and three daughters (who died). He fared no better in naming his estate than himself. Although he called it Ford Park (after the Manor) everyone else called it Godmersham Park (the name it enjoys today).[5]

Thus did the fortunes of the two great houses in the parish diverge. While the Manor of Eggarton suffered two bankruptcies, that of Godmersham enjoyed two large inheritances. On such chances

49   *Thomas Knight's memorial.*

does the fate of things turn. This chain of events led most surely to the ascension of the one, into the fine estate we know and love today, and the condemnation of the other to the footnotes of history. Within a hundred years the house of Ford was to swallow up and extinguish that of Eggarton – but we get ahead of ourselves.

First Thomas Knight's son (also Thomas Knight) was to buy Eggarton in 1780 (as described in the last chapter). He then married Catherine Knatchbull.[6] There is a plaque, on the south wall of Godmersham church, beneath a striking bas-relief of the last trump bringing down the walls of the temple and inscribed 'Sacred to the memory of Thomas Knight Esq of Godmersham Park of this Parish, who departed this life the 23 October 1794 aged 58 years. He was the only surviving son of Thomas Knight of the same place and the last male heir of the ancient house of Broadnax …'. The collapse of the temple columns above Thomas' epitaph on the church wall rather dramatically depicts the fall of the house of Brodnax. His wife, Catherine, is also fondly remembered and her memorial carries with it a stern exhortation to us all: '… in the family vault are likewise deposited the remains of Catherine, widow of Thomas Knight, who died at her house The Whitefriars Canterbury 14th Oct 1812 aged 59 years, a lady endowed with every virtue and amiable quality that could adorn the human mind. Her piety and benevolence were

4   Perhaps I am being harsh. No doubt the change in name owed something to the inheritance of a bequest (or two) by the fortunate Mr Brodnax (who had to change his name to inherit). Quite what Sir Thomas May, who had only left his money to Mr Brodnax on condition he took over the name, would have thought of Thomas promptly, after spending all his money, changing his name again to Knight, can only be imagined.
5   Other members of the Broadnax clan were obviously more attached to the family name than Thomas. There is a marble stone in the aisle of Crundale church in memory of Anne Brodnax, daughter of William Brodnax – died 1794.
6   The family trees of the Knights and Knatchbulls are much entwined. *See* p.89.

employed to the poor … Her death was like her life, pious and resigned. Reader, think on these things and 'Go and do thou likewise.'

Thomas was an only son, and he himself had no children. The House of Brodnax had lost its vigour and so the line came to an end. Having no children of their own, Thomas and Catherine were delighted to welcome into their household their nephew, Edward Austen, the brother of the novelist Jane Austen. In due course they adopted Edward. Following the death of Thomas, Catherine moved to a smaller house in Canterbury and Edward moved in to the family home at Godmersham Park. On her death in 1812 he took over his adoptive parents' name, in tribute to them, and thence became known as Edward Knight. Edward imparted new vigour to the family tree (*see* p.89) as can be deduced from his own memorial on the north wall of Godmersham church: 'In the family vault beneath are deposited the remains of Edward Knight of Godmersham Park in this parish and of Chawton House in the parish of Hampshire, who departed this life November 19th 1852 in the 86th year of his age … in the same vault is buried Elizabeth his wife, died October 10th 1808 in the 35th year of her age. They had 11[7] children of whom the 9 surviving have caused this memorial to be erected to the memory of their parents.'[8]

By all accounts Edward was a fine and hospitable fellow. His sister, the novelist Jane Austen, and other members of his family less fortunate than he, were frequent visitors to the great house at Godmersham. Indeed, on his real father's early death, Edward was able to offer his family a house in which to live. They were offered a place on his Godmersham estate (perhaps Eggarton Manor) or a place on his Chawton estate in Hampshire. They chose to live in 'Little Chawton'. They were, however, frequent visitors to Godmersham. Here they joined in the social life of the landed gentry in Kent, attending many parties and even taking part in the cricket matches which Edward would organise. Edward was a keen cricketer and his son went on to play for both Kent and Hampshire. Jane catches these social occasions in her frequent letters to her favourite sister Cassandra:

> … it gives us great pleasure to know that the Chilham Ball was so agreeable, and that you danced four dances with Mr Kemble. Desirable, however, as the latter circumstance was, I cannot help wondering at its taking place. Why did you dance four dances with so stupid a man? Why not rather dance two of them with some elegant brother officer who was so struck with your appearance as soon as you entered the room?[9]

She seems to have spent happy times at the house and, for a while, to have enjoyed the elegant leisure of the landed gentry. She wrote on 16 June 1808: 'Yesterday passed quite à la Godmersham: the gentlemen rode about Edward's farm, and returned in time to saunter along Bentigh with us; and after dinner we visited Temple Plantations, which, to be sure is a Chevalier Bayard of a plantation. James and Mary are much struck with the beauty of the place.'

---

7   Perhaps the strain of bearing 11 children by the age of 30 undermined Elizabeth's strength. Edward and Elizabeth are also memorialised in the Eastern windows of the church, behind the altar, inscribed 'to the glory of God and in memory of Edward Knight who departed this life Nov 19 1852 aged 85 and also of Elizabeth his wife who departed this life Oct 10 1807 aged 35.' Poor Edward lived 44 years a widower.

8   Edward Knight's son, also Edward Knight, lived at Chawton House in Hampshire, and sold the Godmersham Estate (including Eggarton) to John Cunliffe Lister Kay in 1874. He was succeeded by his brother Ellis. In 1921 the Third Lord Masham sold the estate to the Earl of Dartmouth. In the mid-1930s the estate was sold to Mr and Mrs Robert Tritton and then in 1983 to the Sunley family.

9   Letter 27 of Brabourne Letters, 14 Jan 1800 or 1801.

The next day she describes a family walk down the lane to visit Elizabeth Knight (of the feeble intellect) at Eggarton, under the care of the Miss Cuthbert sisters:[10] 'I am now just returned from Eggarton; Louisa and I walked together and found Miss Maria at home. Her sister we met on the way back. She had been to pay her compliments to Mrs Inman, whose chaise was seen to cross the park while we were at dinner yesterday.'

Many of the characters in her book must have been drawn from the society she enjoyed at Godmersham; she is supposed to have modelled Mansfield Park on her time there. It is not hard to imagine Jane, at her table in the library, writing of a hero riding across the park to sweep her up and whisk her away from her constrained spinster's existence. Real life, however, for unmarried daughters in Edwardian England was not so kind; perhaps she was only truly free on the pages of her books.

But 'the times they were a changing' and the peace and leisurely pace of the Stour valley was about to be broken by the pre-cursors of industrial revolution. Her brother Edward was a man of his times and, prompted by the increasing traffic from Ashford to Canterbury and the spate of new turnpike road-building by private landowners, he decided to promote a turnpike of his own – straight along the valley floor on the east side of the Stour, from Bilting to the Canterbury-Charing turnpike which passed to the north of Chilham. This would, conveniently, divert traffic from the old road which passed by his own mansion and through his own park to meet the Chilham estate at Mountain Street (formerly known as Mounting Street). The new route involved bridging the River Stour beneath Godmersham church and crossing land belonging to Court Lane Farm, owned by the Dean and Chapter of Canterbury. No doubt the diversion of traffic away from his own property played a large part of his ambition for the new turnpike, but (like any modern day developer) he was not slow to point out the economic benefit that this new road would bring to the farm, as can be seen from his letter of 1830 to the Dean and Chapter of Canterbury shown opposite.

His strategy must have been successful, since the road was built and today still provides the main artery along the valley for traffic from Ashford to Canterbury. He thus preserved both Godmersham's tranquil park and Chilham's medieval village square from the onslaught of 'the infernal combustion engine.'[11]

Although, indirectly, we have Edward Knight to thank for preserving these ancient enclaves he was a destroyer as well as creator. Edward took a lease of Court Farm Lodge (then erroneously known as Godmersham Priory) from the Dean and Chapter of Canterbury in 1835 and bought it, and its landholding in the village, outright in 1850. Edward promptly pulled down some of the old priory buildings. Henceforth the fate of the village was to be more bound up with the secular considerations of the landed gentry than the ecclesiastical ones of the church – as it was to find to its cost.

Edward also seemed to have taken against Eggarton Manor. Some time earlier, after Elizabeth died, it seems Edward did not care to let out such a large manor so close to his own, and so, in 1828, chose to pull it down.[12] This was a sad end to a Manor with such a history and marks the final triumph of the Godmersham estate over that of Eggarton.

---

10   *See also*, for an earlier visit, *Letters of Jane Austen* – Brabourne Edition: Letters to her sister Cassandra: Letter no 24, 20 November 1800 'You and George walking to Eggerton!' The reference to George is presumed to be to George Knight, son of Edward Knight (Jane's brother).

11   As John Betjeman would refer to the motor car.

12   *See* Kent online: http://www.historic-kent.co.uk under Godmersham.

50 *Edward Knight's letter of 1830.*

Perhaps there is some further story to tell about Edward's decision to pull it down, but, if so, I have yet to unearth it. The first Baron Brabourne (a relative of Jane Austen) records its demise simply as follows:

> Eggarton House stood on the East side of Godmersham, in the Parish of Crundale, near a wood which went by the name of Purr Wood, and was eventually pulled down,

> Mr Knight, who did not care to let it, being so near Godmersham.[13]

It seems one parish was just 'not big enough for the two of them'.

There is but one other account of the Eggarton estate which I have been able to find, and this was penned by Mr Igglesden shortly before the First World War.[14] He describes Eggarton as having once been a large and ancient home of a great many rooms, standing in the midst of a small park, and continues:

> The field that now sweeps down to the bridleway was laid out as lawn, and clusters of trees were dotted around the grounds … here and there are bits of brickwork which take us back quite to Tudor times … only a very small part of the place remains although the size and style of the stables gives some idea of the importance and dimension of the place.

He also confirms the original house as having being replaced in the 17th century by a new mansion[15] only to be pulled down by Edward Knight in 1828.

Fortunately for us, not all the buildings were destroyed. The Manor was survived by the old well, an enormous oak beamed barn, our own house (described above as a stable) and another house, which is today referred to as Eggarton Manor (but is really a part, subsequently extended, of the original Manor out-buildings).

Thus was the Manor built perhaps by one Knight and pulled down by another.

Edward Knight (junior), who inherited Godmersham Park in 1852, carried on in the same vein as his father. He took against Godmersham village, which had stood to the north-east of the church, between the great house and the ford, for over a thousand years. In 1852, feeling that it spoiled the view, he moved it out of sight (and site), to the far side of his father's turnpike road.[16] He must have had particularly good eye-sight, since he lived

---

13   *Jane Austen's Letters*, Brabourne edition, annotations to letter no. 24. It may be that the reference there to Eggarton being in the parish of Crundale is a mistake – unless at some stage the parishs of Godmersham and Crundale were combined.

14   *See* Canterbury Cathedral archives CCA-U3-117/28/1.

15   *See further* Chapter 15.

16   The house opposite the Old Post Office has 'EK, 1854' on a plaque above the door. We can surmise

51   *Godmersham Park and village before Edward Knight.*

over a hundred miles away at Chawton House in Hampshire. Thus was the old Saxon settlement lost. Godmersham village, as Eggarton Manor before it, suffered from being 'inconveniently close' to Godmersham Park. Gone were its glory days of market and feast days, gone the self confident merchants who would mint their own money. Removed from its church, sandwiched between the new turnpike (of 1833) and the new railway (of 1846), and bereft of its pub, school and Post Office, the village went into decline.[17]

Not content with moving the village, he turned his attention to Godmersham Park, added new wings to the house, built walled gardens over the old village site, replaced the Georgian windows with Victorian sashes, and painted the whole a dreary battleship grey. Having thus, with the benefit of large sums of money, vandalised the property, he chose not to live there – and let it out.

---

therefore that Edward Knight cleared out the village two years after he first became its landowner in 1852.

17   It is possible that, prejudiced by the destruction of our own Manor at Eggarton, I am doing Edward Knight a disservice – and that he believed he was improving the lot of his villagers by giving them new accommodation.

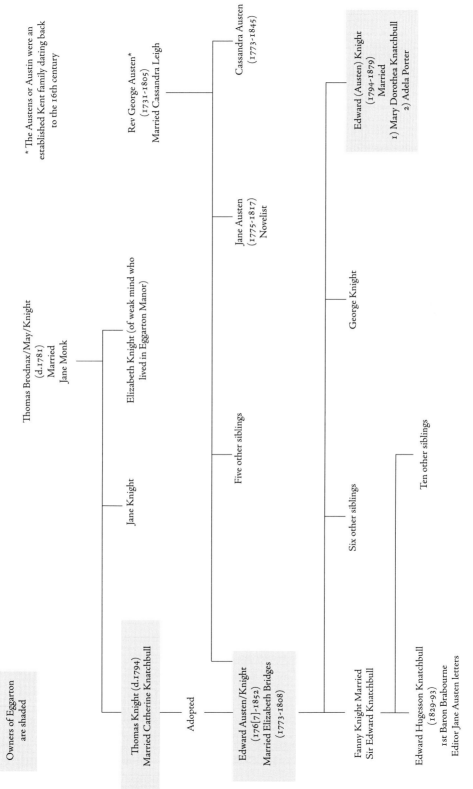

Owners of Eggarton
are shaded

* The Austens or Austin were an
established Kent family dating back
to the 16th century

Thomas Brodnax/May/Knight
(d.1781)
Married
Jane Monk

Rev George Austen*
(1731-1805)
Married Cassandra Leigh

Cassandra Austen
(1773-1845)

Jane Knight

Elizabeth Knight (of weak mind who
lived in Eggarton Manor)

Jane Austen
(1775-1817)
Novelist

Edward (Austen) Knight
(1794-1879)
Married
1) Mary Dorothea Knatchbull
2) Adela Porter

Five other siblings

George Knight

Thomas Knight (d.1794)
Married Catherine Knatchbull

Adopted

Edward Austen/Knight
(176[7]-1852)
Married Elizabeth Bridges
(1773-1808)

Six other siblings

Ten other siblings

Fanny Knight Married
Sir Edward Knatchbull

Edward Hugessen Knatchbull
(1829-93)
1st Baron Brabourne
Editor Jane Austen letters

52 *Knight Austen family tree.*

XVII

Cunliffes, Kays and Listers

Eggarton meets the Industrial Revolution

The Old Series Historical Map, 1813-19,[1] depicts Eggarton in a distinctive square shape, consistent with the lay-out of a manor house and attendant buildings around a courtyard. By the time the 1876 map was drawn up, however, the bottom (west) side of the square had gone (the Manor having been pulled down) and the settlement renamed 'Great Eggerton Farm'.

Around this time, many parts of England underwent massive growth, galvanised by the new technologies of the industrial revolution. Godmersham and Eggarton, however, went into decline. In ancient and medieval times Eggarton was at the crux of things, but then the focus of events moved elsewhere, and Eggarton become a backwater. The great manor house disappeared, lost beyond memory.

Notwithstanding this gentle decline, the story of Eggarton was, once again, to become bound up with the changes sweeping the country, when it encountered one of the driving forces of the industrial revolution. In 1874 Edward Knight (the son of the Edward Knight who demolished the manor) sold the Godmersham estate (including Eggarton) to John Cunliffe Kay of Manningham, Yorkshire. The Cunliffes, like the Brodnax/Knight/Austen family before it, found it unnecessary to confine themselves to a single family name. The patriarch of the family, Ellis Cunliffe (1774 to 1853), like Thomas Brodnax, acquired three family names (and three wives as well). Beginning life as Ellis Cunliffe, he married an heiress, Ruth Lister, and changed his name to Ellis Cunliffe Lister. Following her death, he found another lady of property to marry, Mary Kay. He added her estate and name to his own, becoming Ellis Cunliffe Lister Kay. Following her death he married again but, finding three wives and four names sufficient, he remained as Ellis Cunliffe Lister Kay. He did, however, have five sons and four daughters, all of whom were Cunliffes, some of whom, as the fancy took them, were Cunliffe Listers or Cunliffe Kays or Lister Kays, and one

---

1   Cassini map 189 'Ashford and Romney Marsh'.

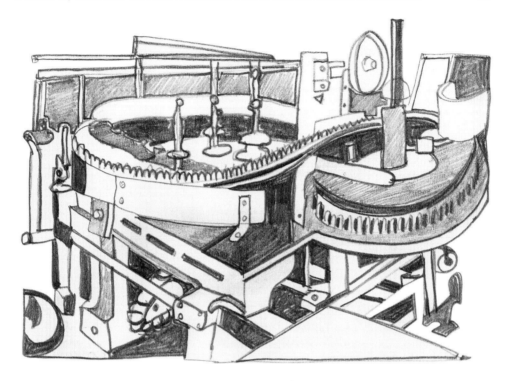

53   *Samuel's comb.*

of whom was a Cunliffe Lister Lister-Kay. This family therefore represents something of
a challenge to the genealogist; nevertheless an abbreviated family tree (as best as can be
managed) follows at p.92 – accuracy not guaranteed.

The Cunliffe Listers of Manningham were an old Yorkshire family.[2] Ellis Cunliffe
became Bradford's first member of parliament in 1832 when it became a parliamentary
borough. John Cunliffe, who bought the Godmersham estate, was the fourth[3] of Ellis' five
sons; his fortune was caught up with that of his younger brother Samuel Cunliffe Lister
to whom we now turn.

Samuel Cunliffe Lister was born in 1815, six months before the battle of Waterloo; he
was to become one of the great inventors of his day, patenting over 150 inventions. His
father, Ellis, established Samuel and his brother John in business in 1836 and built them
a mill for the weaving of worsted. Samuel immediately turned his mind to the design of
various ingenious inventions to improve production and became the first man to create a
machine for the combing of wool[4] prior to its spinning and weaving. This transformed the
woollen industry and enabled him to build an empire of worsted factories across England,
France and Germany.

Samuel was a man of prodigious energy as well as invention. Looking one day at the left-
over remains from the silk spinning business (known as 'chassum') he determined to find
a method to turn this into thread. When Samuel turned his mind to something he would

---

2   Originally from Lancashire, and dating back to Adam de Cunliffe, 1282.
3   Some sources suggest he only had fours sons – but this appears incorrect.
4   Combing involved separating wool into parallel strands and laying them flat.

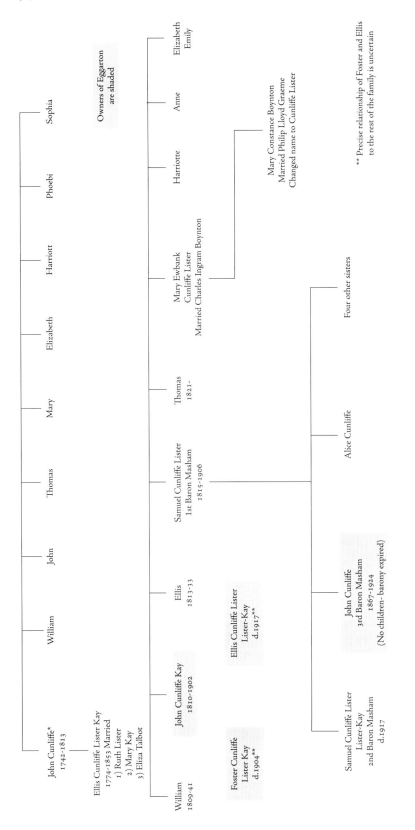

54 *Cunliffe Lister Kay family tree.*

not let it rest. He pursued this idea for 20 years, spending all his considerable fortune on it[5] and bringing himself to the brink of bankruptcy. His endeavours finally paid off, however, and he created a combing machine to dress the silk, thus offering proof to the old northern saying: 'where there's muck there's brass.'

With his Midas touch Samuel turned refuse into gold and went on to create an even greater fortune than before. Two great inventions and fortunes would have satisfied lesser men; Samuel, however, went on to create a new type of loom, this time for velvet, thus making plush (and another fortune) along the way. He went on to became High Sheriff of Yorkshire in 1887, and was elevated to the peerage in 1891 as the First Baron Masham of Swinton.

He donated a fine park to the people of Bradford (who erected a statue in his honour) and found the time meanwhile to invent an airbrake for the railways. He was a man for whom anything was possible – one of those fine breed of Victorians whose energy and ingenuity changed the world and, for a while, gave Britain a pre-eminent place in it. He died in 1905 at the fine old age of 91, leaving behind him a business worth over two million pounds.

Baron Masham was a much respected benefactor when he died, and went some way to improving working conditions in his factories, but in his earlier days as a mill-owner his industrial relations were not always so good. One Christmas he sought to reduce the wages of 1,100 of his mill workers by 25 per cent; those who refused to accept this were locked out and so, in solidarity, 5,000 workers downed tools and went on strike. Four months later hunger and poverty forced them back to work. The ramifications went deep, however, as the workers from his Manning Mills banded together to form the Bradford Labour Union; this went on to become the Independent Labour Party which went on to become today's Labour Party. In 1926 one of his relatives, Philip Cunliffe Lister, was President of the Board of Trade and, with Stanley Baldwin, faced down the TUC over the General Strike. Subsequently another relative, David Cunliffe-Lister, was Margaret Thatcher's Chief Whip in the House of Lords when she took on and defeated Arthur Scargill's miners in the strike of 1982. The Cunliffe family thus 'had form' when it came to industrial disputes. It remains, however, one of history's little ironies that the First Baron was, in his way, responsible for the founding of the Labour movement and, despite the efforts of his descendants, their ultimate rise to power and government.

Meanwhile, back in the 19th century, some of the First Baron's fortune rubbed off on his brother and business partner: John Cunliffe Kay. With it, John purchased the Godmersham Estate from Edward Knight for £225,000 in 1874. It seems he had no immediate use for Eggarton Farm, however, which was listed as 'Uninhabited' in the 1881 census. He was a benevolent landlord to the village, building a school for its children in 1883. John died in 1902 and is buried just outside the eastern wall of Godmersham church. At this time his school was one of only two left in the country retained by private individuals.[6] He left the estate to his cousin Foster Cunliffe Lister Kay, who enjoyed it for just two years before himself dying in 1904 and passing it on to his cousin Ellis Cunliffe Lister Lister-Kay (a man for whom, in a name, just one Lister was not enough).[7]

---

5   £350,000 – a king's ransom in those days.
6   His gravestone reads: 'In memory of John Cunliffe Kay of Godmersham Park who died the 28th day of November 1902 and of his wife Anne who died the 13th day of March 1898 in her 78th year.'
7   Although the title deeds to the Eggarton property show title passing from John to Foster Cunliffe Lister

Perhaps money became a little tight after the First Baron's death; at any rate, the estate was mortgaged in 1906 for £30,000.

1917 was a bad year for the family. While the Great War raged on Ellis died, in March, leaving Eggarton in his will to his cousin Samuel, the Second Baron Masham (son of the First Baron, the great inventor – *see* family tree at p.92). Samuel Cunliffe Lister Lister-Kay did not inherit his father's commercial bent, preferring art to business. Nor did he inherit his father's robust constitution. Nor in fact did he inherit his brother Samuel's estate – since he died of a heart attack two months before him, without wife or issue. The estate therefore passed to his sister Alice. Alice decided she had no use for it (perhaps the £30,000 mortgage had something to do with this) and passed it on to her brother John Cunliffe, who had become the 3rd Baron Masham after his brother's death in January. John was a great sportsman; he climbed the Matterhorn before he was 18 years old. Sadly, he too had a fatal weakness and died of a heart attack in 1924, leaving no issue. John however had at least paid off the mortgage, in 1918, and had sold the Eggarton estate in December 1920 to Henry Mandy Simmons before he died.

As the estate passed from one Lister-Kay to another at the beginning of the 20th century, the country descended into the nightmare of war. Once again national events left their mark on the estate. Towards the end of 1914 the Germans embarked on a submarine campaign against our merchant shipping fleet, hoping to destroy our supplies and starve Britain into surrender. The big lumbering convoys were easy meat for the U-boat packs. At the height of the campaign a merchant-man went to the bottom, on average, once every 36 hours. Something had to be done. The Admiralty needed a means of spotting the German U-boats and decided that air-ships were the answer. Godmersham, with its expansive park, offered open space for the giant vessels to take off and land, while its wood provided ideal camouflage for them when not in use. As may be imagined, concealing two leviathans some 143 feet long and 32 feet in diameter, was no easy task. Accordingly a great pit 30 feet deep was dug in King's Wood to shelter them. The depression left by this pit can still be seen today in the slopes above Godmersham Park at the south-western end of the estate near the Pilgrim's Way.

Thus in September 1914 Godmersham became host to a Parseval Class Airship – one of only three available and, ironically, German-built, by Major August Von Parseval. It seems somehow fitting that his invention was first trialled, in 1909, at the Gordon Bennett Balloon race at Zurich. It is quite clear, however, that the serious-minded Major August Von Parseval shared few of the traits of the flamboyant playboy Gordon Bennett (junior) who ran the race.[8]

Kay and then to Ellis Cunliffe Lister Kay, I have not been able to establish the precise relationship they bear to each other. The names became so confusing, I wonder if they themselves knew. I have been able to find details of a Sir Foster Hugh Egerton Cunliffe 6th Baronet of Liverpool, who died in the First World War in 1916 without wife or issue. The Liverpool Cunliffes were a related branch of the family, but if this is the same person as the Foster who briefly owned Eggarton, he may have been dismayed to find that the rest of the family clearly thought him dead for the previous 12 years. Nigel Nicolson in his booklet, 'Godmersham Park Kent' (written following the rediscovery of the 1874 sale particulars of the estate) writes that John was succeeded by his brother Ellis, and Ellis' two sons. A sister publication 'Godmersham Park – A Short History' states that 'John … was eventually succeeded by his brother Ellis, who became the First Lord Masham'. If this is correct, then it seems the great man himself became owner of the estate, but must have changed his names from those in the family tree on p.92.

8   James Gordon Bennett (junior), 1841-1918, was the son of a New York Newspaper magnate of the same name. His passion for trains, planes and automobiles, fast cars and fast women (not to mention balloons) gives

55   Colonel Field's sketch of the airship hole.

= original shape of Airship hole

By 1918 Godmersham Park was host to two English-built Zero Class Airships. It offered a mooring-out station to RNAS[9] Kingsnorth, near Ashford, which became the most important airship base in the country. It had two enormous hangars for its ships – one 700 feet long, 150 wide and 98 feet tall. The monsters housed in these hangars would make the jumbo jets of today look modest. There appears to have been some friction between the Royal Navy and the fledgling Royal Air Force as to who should have responsibility for these balloons. The Navy ultimately gained the upper hand, by cleverly calling them 'air ships', and claiming them for their own.

The Godmersham airships were kept afloat by 70,000 cubic feet of hydrogen, carried a crew of three and, true to their name (airship), had a boat-like carriage slung underneath them. Propelled by a purpose-built 75 hp Rolls Royce Hawk engine, with a top speed of 53 mph and maximum rate of ascent of 1,200 feet per minute, they were able to reach the

---

him claim to be the first international playboy. He sponsored Stanley's expedition to Africa to find Livingstone, won the first trans-oceanic boat race, and sponsored the Gordon Bennett balloon race in Switzerland. Gordon Bennett (junior) may have been forgotten, but he springs to mind again almost every day: 'Oh gawd an' benet'.
9   Royal Naval Air Service.

Thames Estuary or the English Channel in a matter of minutes.

These whales of the sky would take off and return to dock at two long mooring chains, 120 feet apart, in a field behind the Manor House, before being moved to safe anchorage in King's Wood; there they would bed down like two great toads in their airship hole. Notwithstanding all this care, one of these Airships (S.S. Zero 5) caught fire on 17 September 1918. The flames would have been seen a mile away down the valley at Eggarton. It must have made quite a sight.

The airships were never the most practical instruments of war. Like the dinosaurs before them, they grew bigger and bigger as they progressed down their evolutionary cul-de-sac, before being overtaken by the smaller and nimbler aeroplanes, buzzing past them like angry gnats. Just as the dinosaurs were doomed, supposedly, to extinction by a massive fireball falling to earth, so were the airships condemned, when the 804-foot Hindenburg[10] (that Titanic of the skies) crashed in its own ball of fire.

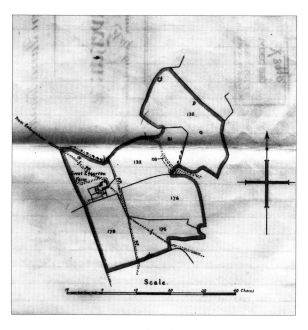

56   *1920 plan of the estate.*

By the end of the First World War, 13 million deadweight tons had been sent to the bottom along with 12,000 able seamen. What we cannot know is how many ships and sailors were saved by the great airships. We do know, however, that they were a great morale boost to the sailors below, who affectionately knew them as the 'battlebags'.

The War to End Wars proved no such thing, and 20 years later the Godmersham airship hole again offered service to its country. Peter Fleming,[11] intrepid traveller, adventurer and, in all likelihood, spy, put a false timber bottom in the hole, and covered it with chalk (*see* Fig. 55). This became the secret headquarters for the resistance effort to be offered by the Home Guard, in the event of a German invasion. It was capable of concealing 60 people.

The Germans have always had a curious affinity for the airship. Count Ferdinand Von Zeppelin, it was of course, who invented the Zeppelin, and lent it his name. Major August Von Parseval, taking up the challenge, gave it an epic Wagnerian scale. The Hindenburg gave it its tragic and dramatic denouement. Or so one might have thought, but the Germans could not quite leave it there. The dream of the airship lodged deep in their psyche and emerged again at the turn of the millennium. They planned one glorious last hurrah, to expunge the painful memories of the Hindenburg, and replace it with the final triumph of German engineering. They would build the 'Cargoliner' – the biggest air-going vessel in the world. To house this they first built a hanger in Brand, South

10   LZ 129 Hindenburg, at 804 feet long and 135 feet tall, was the biggest airship ever built, and was just 78 feet shorter than the *Titanic*.
11   Brother of Ian Fleming, the author of the James Bond books.

of Berlin, 360 metres long, 210 metres wide, 107 metres high and at a cost which bankrupted the company. To give you some idea of its scale, that confident symbol of French ingenuity, the Eiffel Tower, if laid on its side, would fit very comfortably inside the hangar. Alternatively England could lay six Twickenham rugby pitches inside it, and play future internationals without ever having to worry about the weather.

Unfortunately, the expense of building the hangar was so large that they could not afford to build an airship to put in it. The Germans may not have created the largest airship in the world but, as they emerged from their fractious bankruptcy proceedings, they could at least rest safe in the knowledge that they had undoubtedly created the world's biggest white elephant.[12]

After the war, in 1920, at the time of the sale of the Godmersham estate by the third Baron Masham, the Eggarton estate comprised 145 acres, one rood and 33 perches, and was known as Great Eggarton Farm.[13] The title deeds to this sale include a lovely vellum map of the estate, a copy of which appears on page 96. Henry Simmons (gentleman of Eastbourne) bought the estate for £1,870 and immediately sold it on to a company called Eggarton Farm Limited for £3,170. It would seem that Mr Simmons, as well as being a gentleman, was something of a businessman. Quite how he managed to almost double the worth of his property on the day that he bought (and sold) it, remains something of a mystery.[14] John Cunliffe, meanwhile, sold the rest of the Godmersham estate the following year to the 6th Earl of Dartmouth.

57   Lord Masham's 1920 conveyance of Eggarton Farm Ltd.

---

12   The hangar may possibly lay claim to being the largest unsupported (in the physical rather than financial sense) structure in the world.

13   This may have served to distinguish it from Little Eggarton (formerly Little Eggarton Farm), a property lying further up Eggarton Lane, and today owned by Jonathan and Caroline Spencer.

14   Curiouser and curiouser – it seems that that very same year the Company which bought the property, Eggarton Farm Limited (company number 170491), was wound up. Companies House can offer no further information on it.

The First Schedule.

No on Plan	Description	Area.
	Parish of Godmersham.	
91	Rough Grass	6·623
131	Grass	12·289
132	d°	19·665
133	Plantation	·699
135	Rough Grass	40·483
175	Down Pasture	16·113
176	d°	26·489
177	House buildings &c	2·088
178	Arable	21·010
	Total A	145·459

58   *1920 schedule of property.*

1920: PARTICULARS OF THE GODMERSHAM ESTATE

Boughton Corner Farm, Boughton Corner, Boughton Aluph, Kent
Cottages, Boughton Corner Farm, Boughton Corner, Boughton Aluph, Kent
Buckwell Farm, Boughton Corner, Boughton Aluph, Kent
Soakham Farm, Boughton Aluph, Kent
White Hill Cottages, Boughton Aluph, Kent
East Stour Farm, Chilham, Kent
Crundale House Farm, Crundale, Kent
Hunt Street Farm, Hunt Street, Crundale, Kent
North Sole Street Farm, Sole Street, Crundale, Kent
Ripple Farm, Crundale, Kent

Cottage, Ripple Farm, Crundale, Kent
Sole Street Farm, Sole Street, Crundale, Kent
Trimworth Manor Farm, Crundale, Kent
Winchcombe Manor, Crundale, Kent
Little Winchcombe, Winchcombe Manor, Crundale, Kent
Bilting Farm, Bilting, Godmersham, Kent
Bilting Grange, Bilting, Godmersham, Kent
Blacksmiths Shop, Godmersham, Kent
Eggarton Farm, Godmersham, Kent
Eggarton Lodge, Godmersham, Kent
Godmersham Common Farm, Godmersham, Kent
Godmersham Court Lodge Farm, Godmersham, Kent
Godmersham Park, Godmersham, Kent
Coachmans Cottage, Godmersham Park, Godmersham, Kent
Keepers Lodge, Godmersham Park, Godmersham, Kent
Entrance Lodge, Godmersham Park, Godmersham, Kent
Saw Mills, Godmersham Park, Godmersham, Kent
Home Farm, Godmersham Park, Godmersham, Kent
Lime Avenue, Godmersham Park, Godmersham, Kent
Ivy Cottage, Godmersham, Kent
Moorswell, Godmersham, Kent
Popestreet Farm, Godmersham, Kent
Post Office, Godmersham, Kent
The School House, Godmersham, Kent
Village Schools, Godmersham, Kent
Yew Tree Cottage, Godmersham, Kent
Upper Thruxted Farm, Petham, Kent
Brambles Farm, Wye, Wye With Hinxhill, Kent
Godmersham Village, Godmersham, Kent
The Street, Godmersham, Kent
The Street, Godmersham, Kent
The Street, Godmersham, Kent
The Street, Godmersham, Kent
Monument type: Farm; Manor house; Workshop; House; Lodge; Country house; Industrial building; Garden; Post office; School

XVIII

Recent Times

The Estate Breaks Up

Godmersham has never been a large village or a densely populated parish. The eight ploughlands, or farms, referred to in its boundary charter of A.D.824 suggest that it has always had a dispersed pattern (typical of Jutish settlement). It has probably not changed much over the centuries and the original eight farms or hamlets referenced in the charter still probably exist today and can be guessed at as: Bilting, Winchcombe, Court Lodge, Ford (Godmersham Park by the river), Yallande (the 'High Land' at the top of Godmersham Park), Godmersham Common (*see* map on p.82), Pope Street and Eggarton. Hasted, writing in 1798, describes Godmersham village as having 20 houses and the parish as having 240 inhabitants.

It is estimated that the population reached a peak of over 500 souls in the 14th century before being decimated by the Black Death in 1349 when over half the population must have died.

The parish never reached that size again. Despite this, however, it remained, historically, a place of significance. A Gentleman's Magazine of 1810[1] paints a picture of the village at this time as follows:

> The Village of Godmersham consists of but few houses. Here is a long bridge, or rather three bridges, over the Stour consisting of a stone one of three arches, pretty ancient, a wooden one of many openings and a brick one of three; the whole forming a length of near thirty rods. Here was originally a stone one but the last two were added a few years hence to expedite the falling of the water when the arches were overflown which frequently happens in Winter … the Church of Godmersham is situated a quarter of

---

1   *See* Canterbury Cathedral archives ref CCA-U3-117/4/1 – a portfolio which contains a number of pictures and newspaper articles concerning Godmersham.

a mile beyond the village to the left of the road. It is a very plain building of one aisle and a low tower to the north … in the south wall are two large recesses containing the raised pews belonging to Eggarton, the seat of Miss Jane Knight, and Ford Park, the seat of Thomas Knight Esq.[2]

The 1821 census (conducted prior to the demolition of the old village by Thomas Knight and its removal to the eastern side of the new turnpike road) records 414 people as living in the parish of Godmersham (which included Eggarton) in 68 dwellings.

Farm and village life in the Stour valley at about this time was something of a rural idyll, as remembered by Charles Wills, born 1856, son of James Wills, the village carpenter:[3]

> The Downs was a very favourite place for us to go to, for the flowers were many and some rather rare, several kinds of orchis were found there and the views on either hand were splendid; on the right we could see Bilting, Olanteigh Towers, Wye in the distance, Trimworth Manor, Ripple Farm and the hills leading away to Fanscombe Valley and Crundale. Directly opposite were the woods and slopes away over the village and leading to the Old Wye Road to Eggerton and Burnt House and away over the hills to Godmersham Common and Penny Pot (a farm and small hamlet in the woods). More to the left were Pope Street, East Stour Farm with the River Stour running near, right through the valley and Chilham Castle on the extreme left and away (eight miles) the noble towers of Canterbury Cathedral could be seen on a clear day. I believe as many as eight or nine church steeples could be seen at one time if the weather was clear.
>
> The river Stour which added greatly to the charm of our village ran right through the valley from Ashford through Wye past Olanteigh Towers onto Godmersham, where it was spanned by a new bridge near the church and by an old bridge near the entrance to the park and the old village. We boys used to fish in the stream under the arches of the old bridge and up to the sheep washing place where the eels were fine and large, and a few years later I have many times sat on the coping of the old bridge in the moonlight listening to the sound of the Wye bells being rung three miles away, the sound travelling up the valley along the river, then I would wander home, stopping a while near the end of Dodd's home and old Boys garden, to listen to the nightingale, which came year after year to the same spot, just at the top of our garden …
>
> Away to the left was the home farm called the Court Lodge Farm where as a boy I used to go for milk but did not always get it for I have been told they could not spare it they wanted it for young pigs, then I used to have to go to Bilting before breakfast one and a half miles each way … The meadow to the left of the new bridge was known as Long Meadow, and it was very long. I have seen eight men at work cutting the grass for hay, all working one just behind the other; a prettier sight could not be seen than the eight scythes going together and keeping stroke, the stone rubber for sharpening being carried at the back of each man in a leather holder fastened by a belt round his waist.
>
> The half-gallon stone jars were nicely tucked away under the hedge and buried under the grass already cut to keep them cool. At the top of this meadow was the quiet deep stretch of the river where the village boys used to bathe and the further bank of the river was shaded by osiers and willows overhanging the stream; these willows were always a favourite spot of mine for the many warblers, reed and others, used to frequent this quiet spot and the kingfisher used to dart down from his perch in the willows into the stream and away again in a flash.

The most recent census, taken in 2001, records 361 people living in 140 households. The population has diminished and the average size of household has gone down from six to just over two and a half. In the course of this slow decline Godmersham lost its pub, *The Knight's Arms*, a name harking back to the Dukes of Valence perhaps, its school, in 1946, and its shop

---

2 The road referred to here is the old road passing Godmersham Park (the current road not having been built yet). Godmersham church is described in its dilapidated condition prior to its restoration.
3 Taken from a copy of a manuscript typed by the author's grandson, Duncan Moore, and presented to the Rev. Brade-Birks, then Vicar of Godmersham, in 1957; now in the Godmersham estate records.

and post-office in 1982. Perhaps today, however, Godmersham can look forward to a small renaissance having just raised the money for a new Village Hall[4] and built eight new homes by the railway bridge, reserved for persons of the parish and its neighbours.

Fortunately the estate ended up in more sympathetic hands after it passed away from the Knights to the Cunliffes, to the Earl of Dartmouth and then, in the mid-1930s, to Mr and Mrs Robert Tritton. The Trittons restored the house to its former glory with great care and attention. Taking down all the bricks from the southern façade, they painstakingly turned them round, grey side in, and rebuilt the manor, restoring the lovely muted hues of the original. Thus Godmersham Park stands today in its beautiful park, under the careful stewardship of the Sunley family, much as it did in Jane Austen's time, and it is not hard to imagine Darcy galloping up the long ride to the pillared portico in search of his bride.[5]

As for Eggarton, a look at its title deeds reveals an accelerating rate of change in the 20th century. In earlier times there was continuity to the stewardship of Eggarton – a sense that its owners had inherited the estate from their forbears and held it on trust for their descendents. The Manor could stay within a family for centuries at a time. It was passed down from generation to generation in accordance with the laws of testament not the laws of commerce; it changed because it was 'willed' not sold. Geographical and social mobility was limited in medieval times, and children normally lived in the place where they were born. It was not until the end of the 19th and the 20th centuries, with the greater prosperity and mobility which the industrial revolution brought, that the pace of change picked up.

There were more mortgages and sales of the Eggarton estate in the last century than in the previous six put together. Mr Simmons of Eastbourne even managed to buy and sell the property in a single day in 1920! Property had become a commodity to be bought, sold or offered as security, rather than an inheritance to be passed on. Accordingly the estate was broken up and progressively sold off; Eggarton once again reflected in microcosm the changing face of society across the country. The increasing affluence of the people, and the pressure which an expanding population put on the countryside, took their toll on Eggarton.

Today the pressure is greater than ever. The very meaning of the word 'estate' has changed. Formerly an estate would be an area of land, surrounding a manor, under the ownership of a single family. Today it is more likely to comprise a number of homes packed closely together in a single housing development. The modern estates of today are built on the ancient estates of yesterday, and they are more likely to be the creatures of commercial developers than of established families.

In 1924, in the midst of the Great Depression, the Eggarton estate was mortgaged to The National Provincial Bank. In 1926 the mortgage was redeemed and in 1927 the estate was sold to Reginald William Clifford Smith[6] for £2,750. Perhaps this marked the end of Eggarton's days as a working farm. Reginald, in any event, immediately mortgaged it to, who else: The National Provincial Bank. Mr Clifford Smith lived at Eggarton with his

4   Sponsored in no small part by the Sunley Foundation and John and Fiona Sunley. Sadly, since writing this chapter, John Sunley has died.
5   Were he to do so today, however, he would find the building housed an ophthalmic college.
6   Surprisingly, he is named in the conveyance as being 'of Eggarton Farm', so Mr Clifford Smith must have already lived at Eggarton before the company sold it to him. Perhaps Mr Clifford Smith owned the company. Nevertheless, the arrangements behind Eggarton Farm Limited's purchase, from Mr Simmonds in 1920, of a £1,870 estate for £3,170, and subsequent sale for £2,750 in 1927, to Mr Clifford, a man who already lived on it, are curious.

59   *Eggarton lodge and barn.*

wife Dorothy Clifford Smith (née Nepean), and had two children: Cecilia Gwyneth and Edward Reginald Clifford Smith.

When Mr Clifford Smith got married (in 1913, on the eve of the First World War) a marriage settlement was made. In 1940 (in the midst of the Second World War) there was a rearrangement of the trust; monies were advanced from the trust and a mortgage granted to it over the estate. In 1948, after the war, a second mortgage was taken. Thirteen years later (in 1961) Mr Clifford Smith died and the estate was passed on, in trust, to his children Edward and Gwyneth. Gwyneth went on to marry Timothy Reginald Demery.

English Heritage recognised the historical value of the Eggarton estate, and in 1972 they protected the ancient well and wheel-house[7] and the remains of the manor[8] and the old tithe barn,[9] with Grade 2 listings. Fig. 59 is taken from the west side of what would have been the original manorial courtyard, looking up towards our house. On the left you can see the remaining part of the manor buildings and on the right you can see the end of the tithe barn. The original manor, which would have stood back from where the photographer is standing, is no more; it was torn down nearly 200 years ago, as being 'inconveniently close' to Godmersham Park. All that remains is a low flint wall, with the remains of a fireplace in it. Its place today is taken by a swimming pool. There was no English Heritage to protect it in 1828 when Edward Knight took against it.

The listing failed to save the tithe barn. In 1972 Mrs Demery applied for permission to pull the barn down, was refused, but managed to overturn the decision on appeal. Thus the barn, like the Manor before it, was consigned to the dustbin of history, leaving behind only the lodge (our house), the well, the well-house, and the remaining house next to it – now called the Manor.

There were further mortgages, postponement of mortgages and releases of mortgages until, in 1981, Mrs Demery's brother Edward Clifford Smith died. The estate was partitioned and in 1984 the remaining 15 acres, including the last of the manor buildings (and our lodge),[10] was sold by Mr and Mrs Demery, and Edward Peter Demery, to Brian and Sheila Alexander. Old Mrs Demery moved down to Sawpit Cottage at the Western end of the estate.[11]

Set out above is the map from the 1984 title deeds, with all the buildings clearly outlined including, somewhat surprisingly, the tithe barn (which had by this time been demolished).

7   English Heritage ref TR 0754050619 describes it as a 17th- and 18th-century wheel house and donkey wheel, timber framed and clad in red brick.
8   English Heritage ref TR 05 SE 102 describes it as a 17th-century manor house, altered in the 18th century, with a 20th-century extension.
9   English Heritage listed ref TR 06 SE 100.
10   But excluding the building known as Sawpit Cottage to the south of the estate.
11   Now owned by Geoff and Lindsey Oldham, who kindly let me study the title deeds to the property.

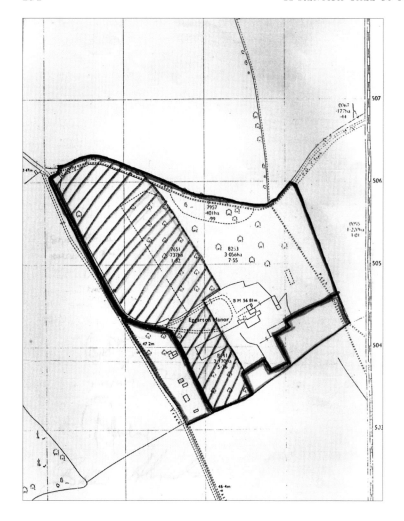

60   *1984 plan of the estate.*

It is instructive to note that shortly after the Great War (with the country entering into the Great Depression) the estate, with its 145 acres, was sold for £1,870. Just over 60 years later, in 1984, the rump of the estate (just one ninth of its former size) was sold for £180,000 – 96 times the former price. This implies a rate of inflation (acre for acre) of a staggering 889 per cent, which goes to prove the old adage: 'Invest in land my boy. They're not making it any more.' If Eggarton Lodge, our own home, does as well, when we pass away our children will be half way to becoming billionaires.

Sheila Alexander (née Lewis) lived in the Manor with Antonia, her youngest daughter, until very recently.[12] Annabelle, Sheila's sister, married the 13th Viscount Massereene[13] and lived three miles away, on the far side of the River Stour, in Chilham Castle. The giant cast-iron radiator, which stands in our sitting room and keeps us warm in winter, comes from there. From the ridge above our house you can see the Castle.

---

12   Editorial note: sadly, since researching this chapter, Sheila Alexander has died. She was buried in the graveyard at Godmersham church on 31 October 2008. Her daughter Antonia Ridell-Martin now lives there.
13   John Clotworthy Talbot Foster Whyte-Melville Skeffington, 13th Viscount Massereene and Baron of Loughneagh, 6th Viscount Ferrard and Baron Oriel of Collon in Ireland and Baron Oriel of Ferrard in the United Kingdom.

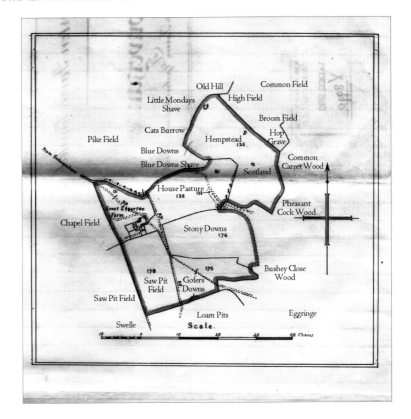

61 *The old field names.*

People remember old Mrs Demery going for a walk up the lane and saying 'I'm just going up to Scotland – see you later.' They put it down to the eccentricity of a lady getting on in years. Twenty-five years later, however, when Sheila Alexander's daughter, Antonia, was clearing out an attic cupboard in the Manor, she came upon a dusty forgotten map. On it were written the old country names of the surrounding fields and woods, remembered as part of the folk lore of the valley; what should the field at the top of the lane be called but – Scotland. Reproduced above is a plan of the 1920 estate with these names inscribed upon it. In addition to visiting Scotland Mrs Demery, on an energetic day, could have done a round trip past such landmarks as Gofers Downs, Stony Downs, Blue Downs, Pike Field, Saw Pit Field, Cats Burrow Shave, and Little Mondays Shave. If not for Mrs Demery and her map, these names might pass away – and we would be the poorer for it.

XIX

CHILHAM

The Castle

Situated a valley away, Chilham, like Eggarton, has roots stretching way back into history. Somerset de Chair[1] describes it thus:

> from the downs across the valley, you may see an English village in all its stages of historical growth, spread before you in a pleasing panorama: the Norman keep, the church, the Jacobean mansion, the Georgian vicarage and, clustered around them, the russet roofs of the old houses around the Square. You will travel the length and breadth of England before you stumble, on a summer's day, upon a more representative example of an English village.

Chilham's history is interwoven with that of Eggarton's. At times relations between the neighbouring manors, and the great families which owned them, were close, at times they were not. Chilham fell into common ownership with Eggarton nearly 700 years ago when the families of Valence (the Earls of Pembroke) and Strathbogie (the Earls of Athol) intermarried.

The manor stands beside a Norman keep, above Anglo-Saxon footings, atop Roman foundations. It is believed that Julius Caesar built a fort here in 54B.C., choosing the position for its commanding view across the river Stour. Subsequently it became known as Juliham, or the village of Julius. Seven hundred years after Caesar, Widred, the Saxon King of Kent, lived there, and it became known as Cilleham – the cold (or chilly) place. Three hundred years later, William the Conqueror conferred the manor on his half-brother Odo, Bishop of Bayeux and Earl of Kent, only to take it back four years later (following Odo's fall from grace)[2] to give it to the Lucy family to hold for the next 200 years.

In the 13th century Richard of Dover, an illegitimate son of King John, transformed it into a major fortress with a stone keep. He was father to Isabella, the 'Comitessa de Chilham' who married David de Strathbogie, 8th Earl of Atholl, a Scottish aristocrat who

---

1   Owner of Chilham Castle, 1944-9.
2   Odo was the second biggest landowner in Britain – second only to the King himself – and acted as Regent when William was out of the country. His power must have gone to his head, however. He was tried by King William for defrauding the Crown, and lost much of his English property. *See* Chapter 8.

could trace his lineage back to King Malcolm III of Scotland (*see* Chilham Timeline on p.109 and family tree on p.110). In 1270 her husband died. She must have had a penchant for powerful Scotsmen, however, for she immediately married an even more august Scot: Alexander de Balliol, Lord Cavers, Grand Constable of Scotland and cousin to King John Balliol.[3] In due course Chilham passed down to her son, John de Strathbogie, 9th Earl of Atholl. It was at this point that their story became connected with that of their neighbours, the Dukes of Valence at Eggarton, with fatal consequences.

Historically there has been a close link between the great landowners of Kent and Scotland – nowhere is this more apparent than in the histories of Chilham and Eggarton. William and his son Aymer de Valence spent a good deal of their time fighting the King's wars in Scotland and (in a conquest of a different nature) married into the Scots nobility, thus adding family connections to their military ones there. Aymer's first sister, Joan, married John Comyn III of Badenoch, and his second sister, Agnes, married Hugh de Balliol. Both families had claims to the Scottish throne[4] and were much caught up in the internecine struggles for the Crown of Scotland. These feuds were a permanent fixture amongst the Scottish clans (stretching back to Macbeth and beyond). Factions formed and changed and if at any time the clans stopped fighting amongst themselves they could be relied on to pick a fight with the English. The Balliols and the Comyns had close family ties and would take one side, the Bruces would take another; the Strathbogies were floating voters favouring one or the other as the fancy took them. This was of course an ideal family for the Valences to be involved with. There was nothing they enjoyed better than a fight and, having thrown in their lot with the Balliols, Comyns, and even, on occasion, the Strathbogies, there was endless potential for this.

When Robert the Bruce murdered John Comyn III before the altar of Dunfermline Abbey, he did not endear himself to John's brother-in-law, Aymer de Valence. The Dukes of Valence were not good people to fall out with, but starting a war with Scotland would have been a tall order even for Aymer. Things became very much easier for him six weeks later when the Bruce proclaimed himself King – an action calculated to stir the wrath of Edward I. Aymer was only too delighted to lead an army north to do battle against the Bruce for his King. This was more than war – this was personal.

Aymer's neighbour in Kent, John de Strathbogie, unwisely chose this moment to change sides and throw in his lot with the Bruces.[5] Perhaps he and Aymer both headed north at the same time. In any event in 1306 these Kentish neighbours found themselves on opposite sides of the battlefield when the two armies confronted each other at Methven. Aymer and the English won the day, leaving the Bruce to seek refuge in the hills and find inspiration in the cave with its famous spider.

John de Strathbogie, 9th Earl of Atholl, and owner of Chilham Castle, having thrown in his lot with the Bruce, was captured on the field of battle. Relations between the two neighbours were now less than cordial. John was brought back a prisoner to Canterbury where he was hung on a gibbet 50 feet high, cut down and disembowelled (with his guts being torn out and burnt before his eyes) before his head was cut off and impaled on the end of a spike. He was not, however, 'quartered' (cut into four pieces); his headless body was burnt instead. This uncharacteristic show of leniency was afforded to him by King Edward on account of his royal blood. No doubt he counted himself very lucky.

---

3   Two years later she died and was buried in the crypt of Canterbury Cathedral.
4   *See* family tree at p.52.
5   His father, David de Strathbogie, 8th Earl of Atholl, had fought on the side of the English.

Having fought against the King he had, in Edward's eyes, committed treason and accordingly all his lands were forfeit. At this critical juncture, when the Strathbogie family fortunes were looking less than rosy, Edward I died and his son, the very different Edward II, ascended the throne.

This change of personnel at the top was seized on by John's son, David de Strathbogie. Somehow David overcame the small matter of his father's treason and beheading and came to terms with the new King. Perhaps he found some common ground – both, after all, suffered from difficult fathers. In any event, not only did he have all his lands restored (including Chilham) he also managed to mend fences with his neighbour the Duke of Valence. He put behind him the little matter of his father's beheading and, to show there was no ill-will, married Aymer's niece, Joan Comyn (the daughter of the man murdered by Robert the Bruce (under whose flag his father had fought, and lost, at Methven)).[6]

Through this strategic marriage to Aymer's niece and part-heir David managed, eventually, to acquire the Lordship of Eggarton. On the death of John Comyn III's son, John, he also laid his hands on Brabourne Manor, thus uniting these three great manors under common ownership for the first (and last) time.

David de Strathbogie, 10th Earl of Atholl, must have been an astonishing diplomat. What his father had lost in war, the son regained (and more) in peace. David's conquest of Aymer's niece, Joan, proved more profitable than any of his father's campaigns. David's fortune having been made by the ascent of Edward II to the throne, so they came to an end with his demise in 1327, when, at the age of 37, David, like his father, came up against someone on the field of battle that he could not talk his way round – father death.

His estate passed to his son, David de Strathbogie, 11th Earl of Atholl, who passed Eggarton Manor on to his kinsman Henry de Hilles in 1334, and Chilham Castle on to his daughter Philippa.

In the course of his wars, Edward I had imprisoned, outlawed and ultimately exiled King John Balliol of Scotland. The remaining Balliols living far south of the border in Kent then found it rather inconvenient to share the same name as the disgraced King. Alexander Balliol of Chilham's nickname was 'le Scot', and so it was that the remaining Balliols changed their name to Scott – and, from 1365 onwards, no trace is to be found of the ancient name of Balliol amongst the family trees of the nobility. The plan clearly worked. Masquerading under this clever disguise they managed to re-establish good relations with the Kings of England and, having successfully buried the connection with the Balliol family, Sir John Scott (of Scotts Hall, Smeeth, near Brabourne) became Keeper of King Edward IV's Royal Household in 1461. So it was that when, that same year, the title to Chilham Castle reverted to the Crown, King Edward IV promptly conferred it on Sir John Scott. His family went on to acquire Eggarton Manor in the 16th century. Thus it can be seen that the Scotts of Eggarton were really Balliols in disguise – and related to the old Kings of Scotland. Confused? Well, that is what the Balliol Scotts, I think, intended.

In a way Sir John (the grand progenitor of the Scott family) can be seen as the fulcrum on which the stories of Chilham and Eggarton rest. He was the six-times great nephew of Sir Alexander Balliol, Lord of Chilham 200 years earlier, and the great-great-uncle of our heroine Dorothea Scott, who inherited Eggarton nearly 200 years later. It is an irony that these Scotts (who were really no Scotts at all) went on to lose their home at the hands of another Scott (who was no Scott at all).[7]

---

6   *See* the Chilham timeline on p.109 and the Comyn Strathbogie family tree at p.110.
7   *See* Chapter 14 and the villain John Scott.

CHILHAM TIMELINE

54 B.C.	Caesar creates a fort above the river at 'Juliham' (the dwelling of Julius) on his second Campaign in England
54 B.C.	Tribune Quintus Laberius Durus, commander of Caesar's legions, is killed in battle and buried at 'Jullieberrie'
8th Century	Widred, King of Kent, creates a wooden fortress at Cilleham
838/851	Chilham (and Canterbury) is sacked by the Danes
1050	Saxon Baron Sired de Chilham is Lord of Chilham under King Edward the Confessor
1066	Sired dies at the Battle of Hastings. King William grants Chilham to his half brother, Bishop Odo of Bayeux
1070	Bishop Odo loses his properties. Chilham is granted to Fulbert de Lucy (Fulbert de Dover)
1170	Chilham remains in the Lucy (styled Dover) family. Robert de Dover rebuilds the Keep in stone
1214	King John stays at Chilham
1207-65	Roese (1207-1265), daughter of Robert de Dover, inherits Chilham and marries 1) Richard de Dover, 2) Richard de Fitzroy (son of King John), 3) William de Wilton
1265	Roese's daughter, Isabelle (by de Fitzroy), inherits Chilham. Isabelle marries 1) David de Strathbogie (1240-70), then, 2) Alexander de Balliol
1272	Isabelle (Comtesse de Chilham) dies and is buried in crypt of Canterbury Cathedral
1306	John de Strathbogie (son of Isabelle and David) is hung and drawn in 1306 at Canterbury. Loses Chilham to Lord Badlesmere of Leeds
1322	David de Strathbogie regains Chilham. He later marries Joane, sister of John Comyn, and cousin of Aymer de Valence
1376	Philippa de Strathbogie inherits Chilham. She marries John Halsham
1461	King Edward IV gives Chilham to Sir John Scott of Scott's Hall (Controller of King's Household)
1551	Sir Thomas Cheney demolishes much of Chilham Castle and uses the stone to build a mansion on the Isle of Sheppey
1616	Sir Dudley Digges demolishes the remains of the Castle (leaving the Keep), and builds a Jacobean mansion.
1944-9	Somerset de Chair owns Chilham (following its annexation by the Army)
1949-97	Viscount Massereene and Ferrard owns Chilham with his wife, Annabelle McNamara (née Lewis), sister of Sheila Alexander (née Lewis) of Eggarton and, later, with son
1997-2002	George Petrou owns Chilham
2002-	Stuart Wheeler owns Chilham. Undertakes extensive restoration

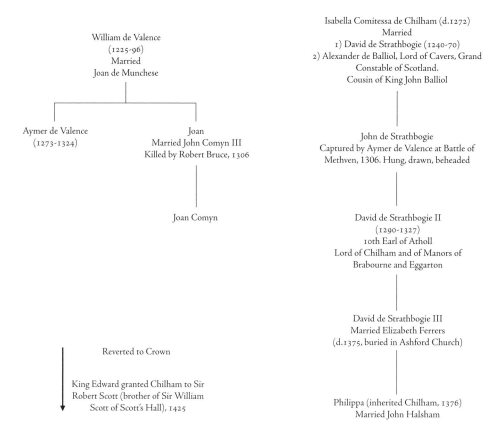

William de Valence
(1225-96)
Married
Joan de Munchese

Isabella Comitessa de Chilham (d.1272)
Married
1) David de Strathbogie (1240-70)
2) Alexander de Balliol, Lord of Cavers, Grand
Constable of Scotland.
Cousin of King John Balliol

Aymer de Valence
(1273-1324)

Joan
Married John Comyn III
Killed by Robert Bruce, 1306

John de Strathbogie
Captured by Aymer de Valence at Battle of
Methven, 1306. Hung, drawn, beheaded

Joan Comyn

David de Strathbogie II
(1290-1327)
10th Earl of Atholl
Lord of Chilham and of Manors of
Brabourne and Eggarton

David de Strathbogie III
Married Elizabeth Ferrers
(d.1375, buried in Ashford Church)

Reverted to Crown

King Edward granted Chilham to Sir
Robert Scott (brother of Sir William
Scott of Scott's Hall), 1425

Philippa (inherited Chilham, 1376)
Married John Halsham

62   *Eggarton and Chilham, Comyns and Strathbogies.*

63   *Chilham today.*

XX

Chilham

The Mansion

In the 17th century, while neighbouring Eggarton suffered the vicissitudes of Civil War, Chilham Castle prospered under the stewardship of the Digges family. As the fortunes of Eggarton Manor waned under the unsteady hand of Major Daniel Gotherson, so those of Chilham prospered under the firm direction of Sir Dudley Digges.

Sir Dudley (1583-1639) had something of the energy of John Cunliffe Lister Kay about him. He was a scholar, merchant adventurer, lawyer and Parliamentarian – a true Renaissance Man. He achieved excellence in all he did, pursuing his commercial interests to become a Commissioner of The East India Company, pursuing his parliamentary career to become a privy councillor, pursuing his judicial career to become Master of the Rolls and pursuing his artistic inclinations to create a gem of a Jacobean mansion. He was characterised by a strength of purpose and an eye for the main chance, together with a certain irascibility of temperament. He was one of the new breed of men who grasped that wealth and position could now be found at the end of the new trading routes. While his predecessors, the medieval knights, may have gone abroad on crusades and conquests, this new breed of man conquered new lands through trade and enterprise. The men of arms, such as our old friends the Dukes of Valence, were beginning to give way to the men of business – lords martial to lords commercial.

Like the Valences before him he realised the value of a good marriage, and married Mary Kempe of nearby Olantigh. She was part-heir to Chilham (and related to the Scotts of Eggarton), and through her inheritance (and his fortune) he got his hands on the ruined castle which stood, so prominently, on its bluff above the river. The Norman Keep was all that was left of a once-proud citadel, the rest of which had been carted off by Sir Thomas Cheney, Keeper of the King's Household in the previous century, to rebuild his ancestral home on the Island of Sheppey.

Sir Dudley was a man of vision and his vision for himself and his considerable family (eight sons and three daughters) did not involve shivering in the damp confines of a 500-year-old fortress. What Sir Dudley had in mind was a life of Renaissance splendour in the finest mansion that money could buy. Drawing on the fortune that his trading expeditions had brought him, he demolished the remains of the bailey and erected the hexagonal Jacobean mansion that we see today.

In order to finance his building scheme Sir Dudley launched trading missions to the far reaches of the globe. He became a Commissioner to the East India Company, led a trade mission to Tsar Romanoff of Russia and sponsored Henry Hudson's expedition to the Arctic to discover the North West Passage. Although he, like others before (and after) him, failed to find a new route to the Orient, he would no doubt have taken some consolation from having Cape Digges and Digges Island named after him. The ship's pilot, Baffin, reserved for himself the enormous island to the north, naming it 'Baffin Island', while the Captain, Henry Hudson, claimed the 'Hudson Bay'. We can only hope that Captain Hudson found some consolation in this when, later in the expedition, the crew mutinied and cast him and his young son adrift in a little boat in the middle of his bay, leaving them to starve or freeze to death as the ship turned round and sailed back to England under its second in command, Thomas Button.

Sir Dudley must have been a broad-minded man (at least where his commercial interests were involved) since he, and his fellow directors of the Muscovy Company, commissioned Thomas Button, accompanied by one of the chief mutineers, Thomas Robert Bylott (after the little matter of his imprisonment in the Fleet had been got out of the way) to lead another expedition to find the North West Passage, and rescue Captain Hudson and his son. Quite how hard Thomas Button and Robert Bylott searched for the man they previously cast adrift must remain a matter of conjecture. Captain Button found no passage to the Indies (leaving this dream to be realised by Roald Amundson 300 years later) nor, needless to say, did he find Henry Hudson or his son waiting for him on the shore of his own Hudson Bay.

Sir Dudley was a man who wanted the best for himself and his family. He employed the leading architects of the day[1] to design his mansion in the latest Italian Renaissance style; when his fine new mansion was ready Sir Dudley moved digs to Chilham. His aspirations applied equally to his grounds as his house. On one of his expeditions he took with him John Tradescant the Elder, the leading garden designer of his day, who brought back with him unusual plants and seedlings for his park. Later Capability Brown created the sweeping views and vistas we see today. Succeeding owners inherited his penchant for exotica from oveseas – a wisteria was brought back from the orient along with, supposedly, a pair of elephants to work the estate. To this day the gamekeeper's house at the bottom of the Park is known as The Elephant House; its two large distinctive arches are supposed to be the entrances through which the pachyderms could pass. Whether these elephants, and their attendant Mahout, were real or apocryphal is still a matter of local debate.[2]

If he had one failing, however, it was his temper. More than once this got him into trouble. Thus it was that at Christmas time in 1626, following some rash words at the Council of State, instead of enjoying his dinner at leisure with his family before a roaring fire in his country seat, he found himself resting 'at His Majesty's Pleasure' in

---

1   Some attribute the work to Inigo Jones – though this is disputed.
2   One of the Hardys, who later owned the estate, does, however, have an oil painting of one of these beasts, and when the house was advertised for sale for £625,000, in 2004, it went under the caption 'So you want to live in an Elephant House'.

one of London's most notorious prisons: the Fleet. Finally he was obliged to swallow his pride and, on 2 January 1627, petition his erstwhile colleagues on the Council of State as follows:

> The unfitting words which fell from him at the Council table arose out of his too much zeal, without purpose to offend. Is heartily sorry for his error, and prays restoration to their good opinions and liberty.

The Council clearly felt, however, that he was not sorry enough and could usefully cool his heels in the Fleet some time longer. It took a second petition, on 23 February 1627, to secure his release.

Close association with the Fleet, however, was no bar to high office. Indeed, perhaps the Council felt that such detailed knowledge of prison life made him particularly well qualified to become Master of Rolls – to which august office he was appointed just three years later on 27 November 1630.

Having built his new home on the foundations of the old castle at Chilham he was thus able to live above the old Bailey in Chilham, and work in the Old Bailey in London. Curiously, just as he succeeded (after some interval, it is admitted) Julius Caesar in Chilham (or Julie-ham, *see* Chapter 4) so he succeeded Sir Julius Caesar as Master of the Rolls in London.[3]

Despite family ties with the Scotts[4] he was not the easiest of neighbours for his cousins at Eggarton. 7 January 1626 found Sir Dudley in the heat of a Parliamentary election and hoping to win a Kentish seat. He wrote to Thomas Scott (father of our heroine Dorothea Scott, and himself a Member of Parliament) in his own particular style, asking him to forward a grossly intemperate letter to Sir John Hippesley, the Lieutenant of Dover Castle, as follows:

> To my worthie friend and Cosen Mr Thomas Scott, Esquire
>
> My good Cosen – If I were not at home like a center of our Motions, and as above to gyve and receive intelligence and directions I should do lesse good then I doe now … to save labour, I pray read this enclosed and then seale it and send it to Dover castle early in the morning, but let a sure messenger in my name gyve it to the Post himself, and three shillings, which I will repay you for the postage – ffare you well, for here come three more letters. Love mee as I doe you, and your honoured hoste's worthie ffamilie, so I rest
>
> Yours ever
>
> Dudley Digges
>
> Sunday 7th, at night.[5]

Poor Thomas only received the letter at 11.00 the next morning, too late to get to the Canterbury Post for Dover. He wrote to Sir Dudley:

> ffor these reasons and others which I shall tell you when I see you, I must either returne yo letters … or keep them a while untille I hear from you agayne. And if you will give me leave, my hartie and ever steadie love unto you perswades mee even to intreate you for while to forbeare or at the least, not to

---

3   The modestly named Sir Julius Caesar (1557-1636) enjoyed a career as grand as his name and became Chancellor of the Exchequer as well as Master of the Rolls.

4   Sir Dudley was related to the Scotts through his wife's Kemp connection – Sir Reginald Scott married a Kemp.

5   Correspondence in the Bodleian Library.

make him [Sir John Hippesley] the sadd instrument of that which I feare may breed you sorrow, who is, and will ever continue

Your true, and most affectionate

Friend and Kinsman.

THO SCOTT

Jan 9 1626.

With the best of intentions he therefore did not forward the letter, and wrote to Sir Dudley in explanation. The next day, however, coming upon Sir Dudley 'in the chamber where the Justices dine' he was roundly abused by him in public, Sir Dudley taking a violent and unreasonable offence at this failure. There is no evidence that this family rift ever healed, Sir Dudley being more than capable of carrying such a grudge to his grave ten years later. Fortunately the penalty for failing to forward letters (even those of a Judge) was not a capital one, and this time (unlike the previous occasion when the owners of Chilham and Eggarton fell out) hanging, drawing and decapitation was beyond the powers even of a future Master of the Rolls.

Having fought throughout his life for the rights of the people, and stood out against the aspirations of the Stuarts to rule by Divine Right, Sir Dudley died on 18 March 1639. Sir Dudley was a man of his times and (notwithstanding accepting a knighthood from King James I at the age of 24) a man of the people. His final work, published on the outbreak of the Civil War, was entitled: 'The Rights and Privileges of the Subject.' His tomb in Chilham church describes his death as an event which 'the wisest men doe reckon among the publique calamaties of these times' – a sentiment which Sir Dudley would have much enjoyed, had he been around to read it.

Chilham weathered the storm of Civil War better than its neighbour Eggarton, and the castle remained in the Digges family for 120 years. Eventually, however, national events caught up with it. As the Digges' fortune was founded on one great commercial adventure, the East India Company, so it was brought down by another, the South Sea Bubble. Thus John Digges, the great-great-grandson of Sir Dudley, lost the last of the family fortune when the South Sea Bubble burst, bringing down the stock market with it. Investors suffering in the great banking crash of 2008 may look back on this stock market disaster nearly 350 years ago and take some comfort from the thought that we have been there before and will, no doubt, be there again.[6] In September 1722 John Digges was forced to sell up to his principal creditor, James Colebrook, one of the new breed of banking barons. Thus ended the Digges' association with the castle.

Sir James Colebrook maintained the estate's links with the East India Company. While Sir Dudley had been instrumental in setting up the Company, as a Commissioner of the Company, Sir James helped take it forward as its Chairman. He also extended the castle's park enclosing 250 acres (out of the 1,000 acres comprising the estate as a whole) behind a tall brick wall. Fifty years later, Sir James' son, also on the verge of bankruptcy (as John Digges had been before him), was forced to sell. The estate passed to Thomas Heron in 1774 when, as local legend has it, several herons drove out a colony of rooks and established themselves in the Park. Thomas Heron, in turn, sold the estate to James Wildman (thus enjoying his estate for rather less time than the herons which he ushered in).

---

6   Individuals may learn lessons – markets, it seems, do not.

At this time, the Austen/Knights of Godmersham Park got to know their new neighbours and were soon on visiting terms with the Wildmans at Chilham. The balls hosted at Chilham Castle were keenly anticipated events in the Kentish social calendar, but this did not give them immunity from the slightly acid tongue of Jane Austen. In her letter of 14 January 1801 to her sister Cassandra, who was staying with her brother Edward at Godmersham Park, she writes:

> It gives us great pleasure to know that the Chilham ball was so agreeable, and that you danced four dances with Mr Kemble. Desirable, however, as the latter circumstance was, I cannot help wondering at its taking place. Why did you dance four dances with so stupid a man. Why not dance two of them with some elegant brother officer who was struck by your appearance as soon as you entered the room?

But Chilham must have had its attractions after all. Later Jane Austen jokingly upbraids her niece Fanny Knight when she writes 'Mr JW [James Wildman] will have you: I see you at the altar … Do not imagine I have any real objection. I have rather taken a fancy to him than not, and I like Chilham Castle for you; I only do not like you should marry anybody.' But Fanny was not destined to be a Wildman, or woman, and became a Knatchbull instead, forsaking Chilham Castle for Mersham Hatch.

The latter part of the 19th century was the time of the great industrial barons from the Black Country. Two of these self-made millionaires from the north decided to buy downland idylls amongst the rolling hills surrounding the Stour valley. While the Cunliffe Lister Kays bought Godmersham and Eggarton, Charles Hardy, an iron-master from Yorkshire, bought the neighbouring Chilham estate. The Hardy's ran the estate from 1861 until the end of the First World War. They were benevolent landlords, in the best tradition of Victorian philanthropy, but their contribution to the renovation of the estate is less kindly remembered. Architectural vandalism appears to have been the order of the day. While Eggarton Manor was raised to the ground, and Godmersham Park was painted battleship grey, so Chilham too suffered in the name of progress. A descendant of the Wildman's commented on the restoration work: 'It is impossible to condemn too strongly the restorations of the Gothic revival.'[7]

In the 20th century Chilham, like its neighbour Godmersham Park, did its bit for the war effort. While Godmersham played host to the navy (and its airships) Chilham accommodated army command. At the end of the war Somerset de Chair bought Chilham as his country seat. He lived there for four years, selling the estate (now reduced to 400 acres) to John Clotworthy Talbot Foster Whyte-Melville Skeffington, 13th Viscount Massereene and Baron of Loughneagh, 6th Viscount Ferrard and Baron Oriel of Collon. The Viscount married Annabelle Kathleen Lewis, daughter of Henry D. Lewis of Combwell Priory in Kent, and sister of Sheila Alexander (née Lewis) our neighbour at Eggarton Manor. For a while, the estates of Chilham and Eggarton were again united by family ties as they had been over 600 years ago with the Strathbogies. The Viscount did much to renovate the estate and, during his time at Chilham, local residents much enjoyed the medieval pageants and parties which took place in the grounds of the castle.

The Viscount died in 1995. Today the estate is owned by Stuart Wheeler, founder of the IG (spread betting) Index, who has continued the work of restoration on the mansion with great care.

---

7   In truth, the castle and house escaped the worst of these good intentions, but the east end of Chilham church, and its attendant family monuments, was sadly demolished and rebuilt.

XXI

Eggarton Today

Alexanders and Ballingalls

When Sheila Alexander and her husband moved to Eggarton from County Kildare in Eire they needed a stable for the race-horses which they bred, and so they built a new timber barn for them next to our house. Although it is a fine building of its type, and much appreciated as a gym by our own three boys, one cannot help but rue the loss of the long tiled roof and oaken trusses of its predecessor.

The medieval well also remains, sunk 120 feet down into the chalk. In former times it supplied water to the tables of the Dukes of Valence and their descendants; today it plays host to a monthly visit from the South East Water company who are interested in tables of a different kind, and who tell, from their readings, the levels of the great aquifers in the Downs beneath our feet. The well is protected by a tiled well house, with a mossy roof, and a huge sycamore with branches rising 100 feet into the sky, and with roots sunk deep into the chalk. The tree, planted two centuries ago, perhaps by a Knight or Austen, is the guardian of the well. When the tree falls it may take the remains of the manor and well with it.

Beside the well stands a wooden donkey-wheel with a massive spindle suspending a bucket, from a rope, over the void. It is 15 feet in diameter and three feet in width. Although it is last recorded as being worked in 1923 it remains perfectly balanced today so that a boy could turn it with the tip of his finger. It is testament to the quality of craftsmen 300 years ago and could not be bettered today for all the engineering technology at our disposal. It is, reputedly, the finest animal-powered wheel of its type in the country. Charles Wills (1856-1929) remembers it as follows:[1]

---

1   *See* Chapter 18, footnote 3.

64   *Model of the old donkey wheel.*

The path across the fields home was a very lovely walk down by the Eggerton Farm; we used to gather primroses, cowslips, violets, culverkeys (as we called them), bluebells, wood anemonies and many others in great profusion. At Eggerton Farm there had previously been a large mansion kept by a wealthy man who used to drive eight black horses to his coach, but the mansion had been pulled down. The old farm buildings remained, and a man named Cole looked after the farm; he had a colley sheepdog. This dog had the strange habit of going to sleep flat on his back with his four legs sticking up like the posts of an old four poster bedstead. In the well-house near was a very deep well. I have dropped stones down and waited in awe for what seemed a long time for the stone to strike the bottom. The bucket was raised by a large wheel built up at the side into which a donkey could step between the spokes and then he would walk round inside the wheel trying to climb the wheel which of course revolved as he stepped, and that worked the rope which brought the bucket to the surface. The adjoining farm was held by Mr Gambrill, an old man whose motto was always 'prevention is better than cure'; the farm was in the parish of Crundale and the church was right away on the top of the downs, clean way from all the houses, buried in a clump of trees. Why it was built so far away I cannot tell but it did not seem that the houses had ever been nearer.

Our own building, the Lodge, was converted from a barn into a dwelling in 1973. It was first lived in by Frank Camier and his wife (who worked for Mrs Demery), then by students from Wye Agricultural College, followed by Toni Ridell Martin, Sheila Alexander's younger daughter (from her first marriage), and, subsequently, by Maud, her elder daughter. Maud Long extended it in 1993, changed its name to Waggoners Lodge and ran it as a bed and breakfast house before selling it to us in 2003. We have changed its name back to its historical one, Eggarton Lodge, and plan to stay here a long time.

Whether our family's tenure outlasts the 250 years of the Hilles, and whether it will again be visited by characters as colourful as the Dukes of Valence, the Rushouts, the Gothersons, the Gotts, the Scotts, the Austens, the Knights, the Cunliffe Lister Kays and all those others who (for better or worse) have left their print on Eggarton, remains to be seen. At least, having delved a little into its history, we will honour its past and serve its future; and if those that came before look down on us today, I hope they will be pleased with what we do. (*See* Fig. 65.)[2]

65   *The old barn in its hay day.*

2   I am grateful to English Heritage for the use of this photo. From this photo it can be seen that its construction was almost identical to that of the great barn at Godmersham Court Lodge.

Epilogue

Eggarton today retains a quiet charm. It has had its glory days and now relies for its survival more on being out of the way of things than at the centre of things. Indeed, while the manor itself and barn have been pulled down, the buildings which have survived have done so by not being too big and grand. Standing in an area of outstanding natural beauty and listed by English Heritage, Eggarton is preserved for the future and protected from the present.

To finish, as I began, I can do no better than some words from that great champion of the Downs, Hilaire Belloc:

> To study something of great age until one grows familiar with it and almost to live in its time, is not merely to satisfy a curiosity or to establish aimless truths; it is rather to fulfil a function whose appetite has always rendered History a necessity. By the recovery of the Past, stuff and being are added to us; our lives which, lived in the present only, are a film or surface, take on body – are lifted into one dimension more. The soul is fed. Reverence and knowledge and security and the love of a good land – all these things are increased …[1]

Thus it is for Eggarton. Its two principal buildings (both pulled down by previous owners) are lost, but not quite forgotten. They can be summoned still. When the mist creeps over the hill or the wind whips up the valley, if you listen hard, you can hear echoes of former days. On the edge of sight, Stone-Age men pick their way silently along the ancient ridge ways, Saxons hide in the long barrows, Caesar's general calls out from Jullieberrie Down, knights clink past Valence Dene, drovers with their sheep make their way through the hollow way at the end of the field, Quakers pack for a new life overseas while Pepys languishes in the Tower. On sunny days Jane and her sister, having left Bath society behind them, walk down the lane in their long dresses to visit their relative – hidden away in the manor at the end of the lane.

Something still remains, and this is its record.

---

1   Hilaire Belloc, *The Old Road.*

Appendix 1
Events Timeline

400,000 B.C.	Stone Age man inhabits North Downs
8,000 B.C.	Britain becomes an island
3,000 B.C.	Long Barrows built on Wye Downs
A.D. 55	Caesar invades. Tribune Quintus Laberius is killed and buried in Jullieberrie Downs
500-600	Saxons invade Kent. Possibly founding of settlements at Godmersham and Eggarton
597	Saint Augustine lands. Converts King Aethelberht to Christianity
824	Beornwulf gives Godmersham to Wilfrid, Archbishop of Canterbury
1323	First written reference to Eggarton, in relation to estate of Aymer de Valence
1334	David de Strathbogie gives Eggarton to his kinsman, Sir Henry de Hilles. Hilles family own Eggarton for 250 years
1574	Henry de Hilles sells Eggarton to Charles Scott for £1,000
1635	Dorothea Scott inherits Eggarton
1642-51	English Civil War
1666	Daniel Gotherson dies leaving Dorothea bankrupt
1680	Dorothea sells Eggarton to Sir James Rushout. Sir James rebuilds the Manor
1780	Thomas Knight buys Eggarton. Elizabeth Knight lives there
1828	Edward Austen/Knight demolishes the Manor
1920	Eggarton Farm Limited is dissolved
1972	Long Barn is pulled down
2003	James and Sandra Ballingall buy Eggarton Lodge

APPENDIX II
EGGARTON OWNERS' TIMELINE

1324	Aymer de Valence, Earl of Pembroke
1324-5	John de Hastings
1325-6	David de Strathbogie, Earl of Atholl
1327-34	David de Strathbogie (son of the above)
1334-1580	Sir Henry de Hilles, followed by a succession of de Hilles until another Sir Henry de Hilles sells to Charles Scot in 1574
1580-96	Charles Scott
1596-1635	Thomas Scott (son of above)
1635	Thomas Scott (son of above)
1635-80	Dorothea Scott
1680-97	Sir James Rushout
1697-	Peter Gott (or Golt)
1735	Maximilian Gott (or Golt)
1735-80	Mary and Sarah Gott (or Golt)
1780-94	Thomas Knight (lived in by Jane Knight)
1794-1828	Edward Austen/Knight – who pulled down the manor in 1828
1828	References below are to the remaining manor buildings
1828-52	Edward Knight
1852-74	Edward Knight (son of above)
1874-1902	John Cunliffe Kay
1902-4	Foster Cunliffe Lister Kay
1904-17	Ellis Cunliffe Lister Lister-Kay (Godmersham Estate Mortgaged for £30,000 in 1906)
1917-20	John Cunliffe (Baron Masham)
1920-7	Henry Mandy Simmons bought and immediately sold on to Eggarton Farm Limited. Mortgaged to The National Provincial Bank Limited, 26 February 1924
1926-61	Reginald William Clifford Smith
1961-84	Edward Clifford Smith and Gwyneth Demery – Edward dies in 1981
1984	Gwyneth Demery (née Clifford Smith) and her husband and son sell the reduced estate (15 acres) to Brian and Sheila Alexander
1993	Sheila Alexander gives her daughter Maud Long (née Alexander) Eggarton Lodge
2004-	Maud Long sells Eggarton Lodge to James and Sandra Ballingall

Appendix iii
1) How Old is that Barrow?
2) The Ancient Kings of Kent

Part i – How Old is that Barrow?

Era	Age	Barrow/Burial	Example	People
Neolithic	4,000-2,000 B.C.	Long Barrow	Jullieberrie, Boughton, Aluph	Stone Age man
Bronze	2,000-700 B.C.	Round Barrow or Tumulus	Eggringe Wood, King's Wood	Beaker People
Iron	700 B.C.- A.D. 50	Hill Fort [1]	Bigbury, Dendge Wood	Celts, Britons
Roman	50-450	Cemetery	Canterbury	Cantii, Romano Briton
Start Dark Age	450-600	Burial Site	Horton	Cantii or Cantware
Saxon	600-1066	Cemetery	Chartham Down, Bourne Park	Jute, Saxon, Angle

---

1   Modern archaeology suggests that the term 'Hill Fort' may be something of a misnomer, with the primary function of these sites being cultural and religious, being used as forts only occasionally in times of tension or war.

Part 2 – The Ancient Kings of Kent

Date	The Saxon Kings [2]
455-88	Hengist
488-512	Oisc
512-34	Oela (Octa)
534-61	Immerick (Eormenric)
561-616	Aethelberht (First Christian King)
616-40	Eadbald
640-64	Encombert (Eorcenberht)
664-86	Egbert I (Ecgberht)
686-93	Edrick (Eadric)
693-726	Wightred (Wihtred)
726-49	Edbert II (Eadberht)
749-59	Aethelbert II
759-94	Aiwick
794-805	Aethelbert III
805-27	Baldred

---

2   There is considerable disagreement over precise dates and names and spellings, and this list does not claim to be accurate.

Appendix iv
Kings and Queens of England

House of Normandy
1066-87	William I
1087-1100	William II
1100-35	Henry I
1135-54	Stephen

House of Plantagenet
1154-89	Henry II
1189-1216	John
1216-72	Henry III
1272-1307	Edward I
1307-27	Edward II
1327-77	Edward III
1377-99	Richard II

House of Lancaster
1399-1413	Henry IV
1413-22	Henry V
1422-61	Henry VI

House of York
1461-83	Edward IV
1483	Edward V
1483-5	Richard III

House of Tudor
1485-1509	Henry VII
1509-47	Henry VIII
1547-53	Edward VI
1553-8	Mary I
1558-1603	Elizabeth I

House of Stuart
1603-25	James I
1625-49	Charles I
1649-53	Commonwealth

Protectorate
1653-8	Oliver Cromwell
1658-9	Richard Cromwell

House of Stuart Restored
1660-85	Charles II
1685-8	James II
1689-94	William and Mary

House of Orange
1694-1702	William III (sole)
1702-14	Anne

House of Hanover
1714-27	George I
1727-60	George II
1760-1820	George III
1820-30	George IV
1830-7	William IV
1830-1901	Victoria

House of Saxe-Coburg-Gotha
1901-10	Edward VII

House of Winsor
1910-36	George V
1936	Edward VIII
1936-52	George VI
1951-	Elizabeth II

Appendix v
Roman Road Past Godmersham[1]

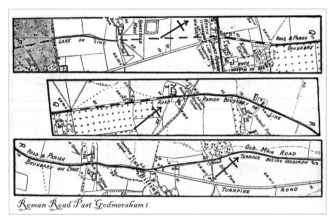

Roman Road Past Godmersham 1

The Roman engineers having steered towards the Stour valley diverted their road clear of the low-lying marshy land by Ashford, heading north east, to the western side of the Wye Gap. This route then strikes out from Bybrook barn, following the gravelly bed of the higher ground a few hundred yards to the north of the present Canterbury road. From here it passes through Kennington to Kempe's Corner (Kempe's Hall marked on the map opposite no longer exists) where it meets the ancient north-south ridgeway, crossing the Wye gap (by Perry Court Farm). From here it follows the main Canterbury road to Bilting where it keeps to the higher ground to the North, behind the line of houses, and past Godmersham church to the gates of the park. Here it turns a right angle to ford the river, cross the main road,[2] and then turns west again down our own Eggarton Lane for a short distance before taking up the line of the railway on Canterbury.

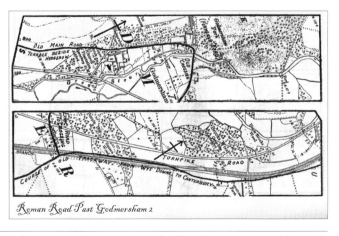

Roman Road Past Godmersham 2

---

1   I am indebted here to the painstaking scholarship and map-work of Mr I.D. Margary and his book, *Roman Ways in the Weald*, published in 1948.

2   Roman roads are often referred to as 'streets' (e.g. Watling Street and Stone Street). In medieval times Godmersham Village was known as the Street; the way south from the crossroad to Eggarton Lane is known to this day as 'the Street'.

Appendix VI

Extracts from The Monk Gildas Bandonicus[1]

504-570 – The Ruin of Britain

Gildas Bandonicus, a British [Celtic] monk, lived in the 6th century. In the 540s, he set out to denounce the wickedness of his time in the most aggressive language. He ended up being the only substantial source which survives from the time of the Anglo-Saxon conquest of Britain. The Anglo-Saxons began arriving in the 470s, originally, perhaps, invited as soldiers as Gildas suggests. By A.D.600 the Anglo-Saxons had control of most of what became 'England' and the Celtic peoples were pushed to the hills of Wales and Scotland and across the English Channel to 'Brittany'.

I. THE PREFACE

1. WHATEVER in this my epistle I may write in my humble but well-meaning manner, rather by way of lamentation than for display, let no one suppose that it springs from contempt of others, or that I foolishly esteem myself as better than they for, alas, the subject of my complaint is the general destruction of every thing that is good, and the general growth of evil throughout the land; but that I would condole with my country in her distress and rejoice to see her revive therefrom: for it is my present purpose to relate the deeds of an indolent and slothful race, rather than the exploits of those who have been valiant in the field …

II THE HISTORY

3. The island of Britain, situated on almost the utmost border of the earth, towards the South and West, and poised in the divine balance, as it is said, which supports the whole world, stretches out from the South-West towards the North pole, and is eight hundred miles long and two hundred broad, except where the headlands of sundry promontories stretch farther into the sea. It is surrounded by the ocean, which forms winding bays, and is strongly defended by this ample, and, if I may so call it, impassable barrier, save on the South side, where the narrow sea affords a passage to Baltic Gaul. It is enriched by the mouths of two noble rivers, the Thames and the Severn, as it were two arms, by which foreign luxuries were of old imported, and by other streams of less importance. It is famous for eight and twenty cities, and is embellished by certain castles, with walls, towers, well barred gates, and houses with threatening battlements built on high, and provided with all requisite instruments of defence. Its plains are spacious, its hills are pleasantly situated, adapted for superior tillage, and its mountains are admirably calculated for the alternate pasturage of cattle, where flowers of various colours, trodden by the feet of man, give it the appearance of a lovely picture. It is decked, like a man's chosen bride, with divers jewels, with lucid fountains and abundant brooks wandering over the snow white sands; with transparent rivers, flowing in

---

1   Internet Medieval Source Book. Author; J.A. Giles.

gentle murmurs, and offering a sweet pledge of slumber to those who recline upon their banks, whilst it is irrigated by abundant lakes, which pour forth cool torrents of refreshing water.

4. This island, stiff-necked and stubborn-minded, from the time of its being first inhabited, ungratefully rebels, sometimes against God, sometimes against her own citizens, and frequently, also, against foreign kings and their subjects.

5. For when the rulers of Rome had obtained the empire of the world, subdued all the neighbouring nations and islands towards the east, and strengthened their renown by the first peace which they made with the Parthians, who border on India, there was a general cessation from war 'throughout the whole world; the fierce flame which they kindled could not be extinguished or checked by the Western Ocean, but passing beyond the sea, imposed submission upon our island without resistance, and entirely reduced to obedience its unwarlike but faithless people, not so much by fire, and sword and warlike engines, like other nations, but threats alone, and menaces of judgments frowning on their countenance, whilst terror penetrated to their hearts.

6. When afterwards they returned to Rome, for want of pay, as is said, and had no suspicion of an approaching rebellion, that deceitful lioness (Boadicea) put to death the rulers who had been left among them, to unfold more fully and to confirm the enterprises of the Romans When the report of these things reached the senate, and they with a speedy army made haste to take vengeance on the crafty foxes, as they called them, there was no bold navy on the sea to fight bravely for the country; by land there was no marshalled army, no right wing of battle, nor other preparation for resistance; but their backs were their shields against their vanquishers, and they presented their necks to their swords, whilst chill terror ran through every limb, and they stretched out their hands to be bound, like women; so that it has become a proverb far and wide, that the Britons are neither brave in war nor faithful in time of peace.

15. The Britons, impatient at the assaults of the Scots and Picts, their hostilities and dreadful oppressions, send ambassadors to Rome with letters, entreating in piteous terms the assistance of an armed band to protect them, and offering loyal and ready submission to the authority of Rome, if they only would expel their invading foes. A legion is immediately sent, forgetting their past rebellion, and provided sufficiently with arms. When they had crossed over the sea and landed, they came at once to close conflict with their cruel enemies, and slew great numbers of them. All of them were driven beyond the borders, and the humiliated natives rescued from the bloody slavery which awaited them. By the advice of their protectors, they now built a wall across the island from one sea to the other, which being manned with a proper force, might be a terror to the foes whom it was intended to repel, and a protection to their friends whom it covered. But this wall, being made of turf instead of stone, was of no use to that foolish people, who had no head to guide them.

16. The Roman legion had no sooner returned home in joy and triumph, than their former foes, like hungry and ravening wolves, rushing with greedy jaws upon the fold which is left without a shepherd, and wafted both by the strength of oarsmen and the blowing wind, break through the boundaries, and spread slaughter on every side, and like mowers cutting down the ripe corn, they cut up, tread under foot, and overrun the whole country.

18. The Romans, therefore, left the country, giving notice that they could no longer be harassed by such laborious expeditions, nor suffer the Roman standards, with so large and brave an army, to be worn out by sea and land by fighting against these unwarlike, plundering vagabonds; but that the islanders, inuring themselves to warlike weapons, and bravely fighting, should valiantly protect their country, their property, wives and children, and, what is dearer than these, their liberty and lives;

19. No sooner were they gone, than the Picts and Scots, like worms which in the heat of mid-day come forth from their holes, hastily land again from their canoes, in which they had been carried beyond the Cichican valley, differing one from another in manners, but inspired with the same avidity for blood, and all more eager to shroud their villainous faces in bushy hair than to cover with decent clothing those parts of their body which required it. Moreover, having heard of the departure of our friends, and their resolution never to return, they seized with greater boldness than before on all the country towards the extreme north as far as the wall.

20. Again, therefore, the wretched remnant, sending to AEtius, a powerful Roman citizen, address him as follows:- 'To AEtius, now consul for the third time: the groans of the Britons.' And again a little further thus:- 'The barbarians drive us to the sea; the sea throws us back on the barbarians: thus two modes of death await us, we are either slain or drowned.' The Romans, however, could not assist them, and in the meantime the discomfited people, wandering in the woods, began to feel the effects of a severe famine, which compelled many of them without delay to yield themselves up to their cruel persecutors, to obtain subsistence: others of them, however, lying hid in mountains, caves, and woods, continually sallied out from thence to renew the war.

23. Then all the councillors, together with that proud tyrant Gurthrigern [Vortigern], the British king, were so blinded, that, as a protection to their country, they sealed its doom by inviting in among them (like wolves into the sheep-fold), the fierce and impious Saxons, a race hateful both to God and men, to repel the invasions of the northern nations. Nothing was ever so pernicious to our country, nothing was ever so unlucky. What palpable darkness must have enveloped their minds-darkness desperate and cruel! Those very people whom, when absent, they dreaded more than death itself, were invited to reside, as one may say, under the selfsame roof. Foolish are the princes, as it is said, of Thafneos, giving counsel to unwise Pharaoh. A multitude of whelps came forth from the lair of this barbaric lioness, in three cyuls, as they call them, that is, in three ships of war, with their sails wafted by the wind andxs with omens and prophecies favourable, for it was foretold by a certain soothsayer among them, that they should occupy the country to which they were sailing three hundred years, and half of that time, a hundred and fifty years, should plunder and despoil the same. They first landed on the Eastern side of the island, by the invitation of the unlucky king, and there fixed their sharp talons, apparently to fight in favour of the island, but alas! more truly against it. Their mother-land, finding her first brood thus successful, sends forth a larger company of her wolfish offspring, which sailing over, join themselves to their bastard-born comrades …

24. For the fire of vengeance, justly kindled by former crimes, spread from sea to sea, fed by the hands of our foes in the east, and did not cease, until, destroying the neighbouring towns and lands, it reached the other side of the island, and dipped its red and savage tongue in the western ocean … So that all the columns were levelled with the ground by the frequent strokes of the battering-ram, all the husbandmen routed, together with their bishops, priests, and people, whilst the sword gleamed, and the flames crackled around them on every side. Lamentable to behold, in the midst of the streets lay the tops of lofty towers, tumbled to the ground, stones of high walls, holy altars, fragments of human bodies, covered with livid clots of coagulated blood, looking as if they had been squeezed together in a press; and with no chance of being buried, save in the ruins of the houses, or in the ravening bellies of wild beasts and birds; …

25. Some, therefore, of the miserable remnant, being taken in the mountains, were murdered in great numbers; others, constrained by famine, came and yielded themselves to be slaves for ever to their foes, running the risk of being instantly slain, which truly was the greatest favour that could be offered them: some others passed beyond the seas with loud lamentations instead of the voice of exhortation. 'Thou hast given us as sheep to be slaughtered, and among the Gentiles hast thou dispersed us.' Others, committing the safeguard of their lives, which were in continual jeopardy, to the mountains, precipices, thickly wooded forests, and to the rocks of the seas (albeit with trembling hearts), remained still in their country.

26. After this, sometimes our countrymen, sometimes the enemy, won the field, to the end that our Lord might this land try after his accustomed manner these his Israelites, whether they loved him or not, until the year of the siege of Bath-hill, when took place also the last almost, though not the least slaughter of our cruel foes, which was (as I am sure) forty-four years and one month after the landing of the Saxons, and also the time of my own nativity. And yet neither to this day are the cities of our country inhabited as before, but being forsaken and overthrown, still lie desolate; our foreign wars having ceased, but our civil troubles still remaining.

110. … And may the same Almighty God, of all consolation and mercy, preserve his few good pastors from all evil, and (the common enemy being overcome) make them free inhabitants of the heavenly city of Jerusalem, which is the congregation of all saints; grant this, O Father, Son, and Holy Ghost, to whom be honour and glory, world without end. Amen.

Index